The Vintage Journey

The Vintage Journey
A Guide to Artful Aging

Trish Herbert

United Church Press • Cleveland, Ohio

This book is not designed to assist people with serious psychological ailments. They should seek professional help. Neither is this book intended to replace legal counsel. Always consult your attorney.

United Church Press, Cleveland, Ohio 44115
© 1995 by Patricia Sloan Herbert

We have made every effort to trace copyrights on the materials included in this publication. If any copyrighted material has nevertheless been included without permission and due acknowledgment, proper credit will be inserted in future printings after receipt of notice.

Printed in the United States of America on acid-free paper
99 98 97 96 95   5 4 3 2 1
Library of Congress Cataloging-in-Publication Data
Herbert, Trish, 1937–
The vintage journey : a guide to artful aging / Trish Herbert.
p.   cm.
Includes bibliographical references.
ISBN 0-8298-1012-9 (acid-free paper)
1. Aged—United States—Life skills guides. I. Title.
HQ1064.U5H445   1994
305.26'0973—dc20   94-35082
CIP

To my
Long-time friend
Canoe buddy
Business partner
Inspiration for how to live and enjoy life
Soul-mate
Kitty Kotchian Smith
1935-1992.
She made an art out of living
and was truly a "walking sun"—
a source of light for all around her.

Contents

Acknowledgements   ix
Introduction   xi
Part 1. This Is Who I Am   1
   1. Integrating Your Yesterdays   8
      Birth   8
      Family of Origin 9
      School   11
      Work   12
      Relationships   13
      Rough Times   15
      Happy Times   18
      Memorable Stories 18
   2. Who Am I Right Now?   23
      Describe Yourself 23
      Feelings   25
      Stress   27
      Religion/Spirituality 28
      Interests   28
      Relationships   29
      Retirement   34
      A Typical Day   35
      Home/Community   36
      Leisure Time   36
      Oppression   38
      Fantasy Questions 38
      Humor   39
   Conclusion   41
Part 2. This Is My Responsibility   43
   3. Values Clarification   45
      Prioritize Your Values 45
      Quality of Life   51
      Values Reflection 53
      How Do Families Start Talking
        About Their Values?   69
   4. Health-Care Planning   71
      Personal Feelings 71

What Makes Life Meaningful for
    You?   73
Resuscitation   75
Artificial Food and Hydration   76
Life Extension   79
Euthanasia   81
Physician-Assisted Suicide   82
Costs of and Accessibility to
    Health Care   83
Conclusion   84
5. Advance Directives   85
    Living Will   89
    Durable Power of Attorney for
      Health Care   92
    Who Makes Health-Care Decisions
      for You?   93
    Conclusion   95
6. After-Death Planning   96
    Preferrences   96
    Funerals   100
    Wills   101
    Life Insurance   102
    Organ Donation   102
7. Financial and Property Planning   104
    Informal Planning   104
    Formal/Legal Planning
      Tools   105
8. Housing Options and Services   110
    Stay at Home   110
    Housing Options   113
Conclusion   115
**Part 3. Self-Renewal: This Is How I Want
to Live the Rest of My Life**   116
9. Meaning   119
    Clarifying Questions   121
    How to Make Life Meaningful   124

Differences Between Middle-Aged
   and Older Adults   126
Peak Moments   128
Practice Simplicity   132
Practice for Living Each Moment   136
10. Self-Care   140
Feel All Your Feelings   141
Unfinished Business   150
Live the Serenity Prayer   156
Learn to Be Still and Center
   Yourself   157
Maintain a Healthy Life-Style   157
11. Attitude   159
Positive Self-Talk   163
Affirm Yourself   164
Reframing   166
Self-Esteem   171
Assertiveness   172

Thriving or Surviving?   175
Mind/Body/Spirit Connection   177
My Spiritual Legacy   181
Universal Lessons of Late Life   183
Self-Renewal Checklist   186
Conclusion   187

Appendix A: Guidelines for Taping
   Your Story   188
Appendix B: The Art of Listening   190
Appendix C: Legal and Ethical Terms   193
Appendix D: Health-Care Terms   195
Appendix E: Sample Legal Documents
   and Responses   198
Appendix F: State Agencies for Living
   Will Information   205

Select Bibliography   207

Acknowledgments

I want to thank my support system: my family, who supply my roots and foundation; Frank Lamendola, my dear Journeywell business partner, who never peeped when I bailed out of work to write this; my friends, who help me know who I am; the women who have attended my "Celebrate Your Womanspirit" retreats; and the many older people I've worked with and known, who have taught me what I know about the journey. I wish to acknowledge and thank the Minnesota Board on Aging for permission to use the pamphlet "Planning for Incapacity" (Orsello, 1990) as the direct source of much of the content in chapter 8. I especially want to thank my dear friend Nancy Randall for her beautiful illustrations in the book and for her uplifting spirit.

I chose to use water lilies as the metaphor for life's unfolding in this book because Kitty, to whom this book is dedicated, and I so often marveled at their magnificence on our many canoe trips together. Like the water lily, we have roots, need nourishment, and must constantly adjust to obstacles and challenges. We are delicate and fragile, yet tough and resilient. We journey upward toward the light and can blossom into fullness, thrive, and flourish.

Introduction

- If you are looking for a practical guide to help you review what has been important thus far in your life . . .
- If you need practical information to know the options to help you plan for a more satisfying present and future . .
- If you want to do what you can to live the remainder of your life as fully and meaningfully as possible . . .

The Vintage Journey: A Guide to Artful Aging will help you in that process.

You are on a journey from the moment you are born. You move through life in cycles of beginnings and endings, experiencing new ventures, changing as you go. The Lakota people talk of following the "Red Road" with the guidance of the Great Spirit. The Chinese speak of Tao as "the way"—revealed and comprehended only by looking at the patterns of your life as they unfold. The Bible is full of journey metaphors: the Israelites journeying out of Egypt to the Promised Land and the repetitive theme of hopefulness in the cycles of loss and rebirth. Most journeys involve leaving and returning. Late life is a time of returning, full of experiences, lessons learned, and gifts to give. It is a time of coming home, a time to look within and make sense of your life.

   The Vintage Journey provides a framework for examining your journey. It is a tool for self-awareness and self-appreciation. This book helps you define quality of life for yourself. You are not only who you are today but also an accumulation of all that you have been before. As you grow older, this realization can provide strength and identity. This guide is not only for people looking at their own aging but also for family, friends, and care givers—nurses, psychologists, social workers, clergy, teachers, doctors—who may need a catalyst to draw out stories and elicit information, enabling them to better understand the storytellers' hopes and potentialities.

   The Vintage Journey is a practical guide to help you explore the depth and mystery of your life. What have been some of the choice moments? The good times? The not so good, in fact, the wrenching, bad times? How did you get through those times? Who were the powerful people in your life—teachers, friends, clergy? To whom have you been important? What are you proud of? Many older persons feel the need to take stock of their lives. The more experiences you have had, the more mountains you have climbed, the better the view. Mysteries and wonders of life are revealed only slowly. What have you learned? What do you need to do now to make the rest of your life as enjoyable and meaningful as possible? Making sense of the journey is a life's task.

Some may think *The Vintage Journey is* "only for really old people and I'm not there yet." Not so. Participating in the exercises in this guide can be beneficial for opening up communication at any age. The book is appropriate for persons who are well into their aging process or for persons who are wondering about their future selves, wanting to be well prepared. It can be the mechanism for a granddaughter who desires to know her grandparent better; it can spark a couple's conversation about hopes and fears; it can be a discussion catalyst for groups; it could be the means for finishing some personal business you have been putting off; it can be used in a very private way, not to be shared with anyone, to review what your experiences have meant and as a means for planning for your future.

Part 1, "This Is Who I Am," reacquaints you with your past, reviews your experiences, helps clarify your values, and assesses how you have evolved over the years. It's a sort of late-life scrapbook, a way to pass along your story. Few things are more fascinating than trying to understand a human life—especially your own. Everyone's story is different. Some stories have more sun; some, more clouds. There are ups and downs, losses and rebirths. "This Is Who I Am" provides a framework for self-exploration. You can participate as fully as you want. You are given the compass to guide your journey, but it is up to you to choose what path to take.

You can't teach a person anything.
You can create an environment in which the person can look within,
unlocking the treasures of the past and discovering the wisdom there.

It is my belief that each of you has your own ancient wisdom deep within you just waiting to be discovered. I invite you to appreciate your life, its beauty and pain, as you would a sunset. By telling your story, you can figure out for yourself what life experiences have been most important to you and what you have learned. Part 1 helps you become aware of your strengths, the ways you have coped, and how you have rebounded from sad events and survived until now. There can be great hope in recalling one's story. You can re-experience the caring in the world, the people who have influenced and supported you over the years.

Part 2, "This Is My Responsibility," gives you a chance to plan and claim responsibility for those things in life over which you have some control. This section gives you background information on your options and defines relevant terms. What services are available that would allow you to continue living in your own home comfortably when you begin to lose energy and health? What factors might determine when you should move? What are your housing options? What do all these new terms mean—adult day care, continuum of care, Elderhostel, living trusts, DNI (do not intubate), DNR (do not resuscitate), durable power of attorney, vegetative state?

What is most important to you? This is your chance to let people know what kind of music you do and do not like, what really irks you, how important certain things are to you, whether you like to be outside in nature or strictly indoors, and whether you prefer to be alone or enjoy the hustle and bustle of lots of people. "This Is My Responsibility" asks questions and presents thought-provoking scenarios that will enable you, and whomever you choose to share your journey with, to gain a clear picture of what you truly value. With this knowledge as background, you then can make your health-care preferences and wishes known informally. Or you may choose to formally fill out advance directives (living will or durable power of attorney for health care) documents that explicitly state your wishes and plans for future health-care needs (see appendix E). Only you have your own answers.

Part 2 gives you the foundational information necessary to plan for your future and empowers you to take some action. Taking responsibility gives you that gratifying feeling of knowing that you have done all you can to make your life as satisfying as possible. It also relieves your family members from the prospect of possible burdensome responsibility and confusion. In addition to helping you verbalize and clarify what quality of life and being treated with dignity mean to you related to health care, subjects such as property and financial worries, funeral preparation, and wills are also discussed.

The last part is entitled "Self-Renewal: This Is How I Want to Live the Rest of My Life." It is about how to live life fully and meaningfully and how to feel good about yourself. Now that you have taken care of planning in part 2, the third section looks at the importance of learning how to appreciate the moment. In the first two sections you will look at your own very special story, your particular idiosyncrasies and values. "Self-Renewal" places your uniqueness in a broader perspective, recognizing your connection with all things, and discusses what late life has to offer and how to take care of yourself.

Everyone lives old age differently. It can be anything. It can be a time of great possibilities and freedom or it can be a time of emptiness and sadness. Particular segments of this guide will appeal to you at different times of your life depending on what you are going through or looking for at the time. By examining your options, doing some responsible planning, programming your mind toward health by expecting to have an old age filled with richness instead of accepting the myth of necessary decline, you can do much to improve your chances of a pleasure-filled old age.

> *For age is opportunity no less*
> *Than youth itself, though in another dress.*
> *And as the evening* twilight *fades away*
> *The sky is filled with stars invisible by day.*
> —Henry Wadsworth Longfellow

The journey is yours.

Using This Book

This is your opportunity to take a pilgrimage into your life. You can choose from several approaches:

1. Choose someone with whom to share your journey. The experience of sharing expands your privacy boundary. You may experience a sense of legacy and immortality.

> *Loving and knowing yourself is wonderfully important,*
> *but being truly known and still loved by another,*
> *the good and the bad side of you, is exquisite.*

Your sharing can be done formally, setting dates for interviewing and perhaps making arrangements for audio or videotape recording. Or just informally pick up the book when you are with another person and find a question interesting to either of you. Try paging through the sections on your own, first marking parts you want to work on and with whom. You need not limit yourself to one person or to any particular number of meetings. Pick and choose what you want to talk about and how lighthearted or serious you want to be.

2. The book can be used reciprocally. Take turns sharing stories, thus building a mighty bridge between you and someone else.

3. You may choose to make the journey a solo endeavor, answering what appeals to you and then giving it, or parts of it, as a gift to someone special. Or maybe you'd prefer talking into an audio or video recorder to permanently record your thoughts and feelings. Directions for taping are provided in appendix A.

4. You may want to concentrate on one part of the book and disregard the others. Part 1 helps you to look at your past and provides a format for telling your story; part 2 gives information to guide you in making decisions about your present and future; and part 3 offers suggestions on how to live your life as fully as possible from this point forward. Skip to the part that interests you most.

5. I created this book because I honestly believe that sharing your story and planning for today and tomorrow is vitally important. Recognizing that you may not have someone with whom to share your story, I encourage you to converse with me even though I cannot be there with you in person. In my effort to make this journey as interactive and personal as possible, I have made myself the other voice in the process by using the opening phrase "Tell me about . . ."

This book is yours. Write in it or have your listener write in it after hearing your response. Some stories, some laughs, some lessons learned need to be recorded and immortalized. Each person is a carrier of an autobiographical novel and it is unfortunate that when a person dies, there is often no way to retrieve the learnings and insights of a lifetime.

When a person dies, it is like a small library burning.
—Alex Haley, *Roots*

You already know that people are so very different from one another. Some of you may have been "searching" your whole life, pursuing the existential questions, trying to figure out who you are, the meaning of this or that, what this life of yours is all about. Some of you are not particularly seeking self-awareness and are pleased enough with yourself, but simply would like an audience for recalling some of your life's special moments. Share only what you want to share. You may have some wonderful tales in your memory that would be a crime not to pass on. You may have secrets you want to keep, or you may have secrets that aren't so mighty any more and find that sharing them can be cathartic and therapeutic. Remember, though, that this book is not designed to assist people with serious psychological ailments. They should seek professional help. Neither is this book intended to replace legal counsel. Always consult your attorney.

The book allows you to step back and get perspective on your experiences, to share them and reflect on what you have learned. You will begin to see the patterns and rhythms of your life and gain clarity about those things you love to do and why. Asked what they would do if they knew that they had only six months to live, most people respond that they would want to express their love to the important people in their lives. They'd like to get things in order, do some long-awaited traveling or other pleasurable activities, and finish up important projects or unfinished business. Since no one knows just when that six months is, *The Vintage Journey* is a tool to help you organize yourself now. The rest is up to you.
Happy journeying.

Part 1 This Is Who I Am

Why do I want to take this journey? The best way to figure out where you're going is to understand where you've been. By deliberately recalling experiences of the past, you, the storyteller, can become aware of the rhythms and patterns of your life and can begin to absorb life's larger meaning and purpose. Telling your story is empowering. It gives a renewed sense of life's significance and dignity. If you choose to take the time to reflect on your life, any one of a number of benefits could occur.

1. This is a guide that helps you take stock of your life. By refamiliarizing yourself with what you've done, what you've learned, you will be able to extrapolate meaning from your own personal odyssey. This can be an extremely healing adventure.

The salvation of this human world lies nowhere else than in the human heart, in the human power to reflect, in human meekness and in human responsibility.
—Vaclav Havel

2. It is an opportunity for personal integration. In *Childhood and Society*, Erik Erikson and Helen Kivnick provide theoretical context for this process and divide life into stages:

Stage	Psychosocial Conflict
1. early infancy (birth to one year)	trust vs. mistrust
2. early childhood (ages one to three)	autonomy vs. shame and doubt
3. play age (ages four to five)	initiative vs. guilt
4. school age (ages six to eleven)	industry vs. inferiority
5. adolescence (twelve to twenty years)	ego identity vs. role confusion
6. young adulthood	intimacy vs. isolation
7. middle adulthood	generativity vs. stagnation
8. old age	integrity vs. despair

Erikson's final stage in the struggle to achieve ego integrity recognizes the importance of integrating and making sense of the various stages and parts of your life, fitting them into a whole. This means acknowledging all of life's experiences, good and bad, and fitting them together into dynamic balance. This reliving of events, the joyful times and the sad times, reintegrates your separate parts. Often it is said that babies are the promise of the world. Yet it is really older people who embrace life, model hopefulness and vigor, who, because they have witnessed much of what life has to give, actually embody the promise.

3. Your personal history is an important part of your identity. It is important to know who you are now, but also who you've been all along. Your past experiences give meaning and continuity to the present. You are much more than who you are this minute.

You can't say a decent goodbye to life until you know what it was.

4. It is a form of legacy. After you die, you will remain in the memories of those who live on. The most common regrets expressed by survivors after someone dies are, "I wish I would have asked him . . ." or "I wish I would have told her . . ." This is an opportunity to share who you are.

> *Stories untold are fleeting.*
> *Stories shared are forever.*

Documenting your highs and lows, your memories of special others and meaningful events, and especially having a record of what you have learned, what has been most important to you, is a wonderful gift to leave to those who follow. Your recorded journey may then become their pathway.

> *What's past is prologue.*
> —Shakespeare, *The Tempest*

Your recorded journey can be the vehicle for transmitting your values, your essence, your hard-earned wisdom to another generation. Something of you will live on. You are the link between the past and the future.

5. It might propel you into action. Perhaps with the accompanying self-awareness from this reflection, you can figure out what you want to change to improve the quality of your life. You have a lot to say about how you age. As it becomes clearer what is really important to you, a sense of urgency may appear. Every moment becomes even more precious.

6. Recognizing your difficult periods as well as the joyous times with all the attendant feelings is an important step toward authenticity. Life review may uncover some deeply buried, hurtful memories. Your gloomy times are a part of you. Sharing your hurtful memories often helps others better understand you and your behavior. Bringing other people into awareness is also useful if it helps you remove a blockage that has prevented you from getting on with life and living fully. Some of you have had smooth sailing; others, rough seas. Most people have some guilt and some regrets about events that did or didn't happen. Late life is a time when fundamental truthfulness becomes more important. Self-acceptance evolves. You stop thinking things will be different than they are.

You gain strength, courage and confidence by every experience
in which you really stop to look fear in the face.
You are able to say to yourself, "I lived through this horror.
I can take the next thing that comes along. . . ."
You must do the thing you think you cannot do.
　　—Eleanor Roosevelt

7. You can't erase mistakes of the past but you can let go of them and begin tomorrow anew. If unlocking memories proves to be too painful, you have the choice to suppress or divert them again or to seek professional guidance to help you understand and learn from the experience. If, on the other hand, you have painful memories that you've worked through, by no means dig them up again. Old wounds are easy to open up; let them be. Move on with your journey.

What we call the beginning is often the end
And to make an end is to make a beginning
The end is where we start from.
　　—T.S. Eliot, *Four Quartets*

No matter how old you are, the adage "This is the first day of the rest of my life" is a great way to start the day. You can leave behind regrets and unproductive patterns and choose to rebirth yourself. You do learn from your mistakes. Lovingly recalling the mistakes and hard lessons learned can be mightier gifts than sharing the successes and the joys.

The past sharpens perspective, warns of pitfalls, and helps point the way.
—Dwight Eisenhower

8. Build meaning into your life. This is a quest to find out more than facts and memories. It is a head and heart exercise. By going back to your formative beginnings, you get to matters of the heart which are often closer to the truth and source of meaning than facts.

This is a revolutionary time. People are living longer and longer. It used to be that, except for rare exceptions, folks didn't age. They simply died. Mid-life, which is now in the forties, fifties, and sixties, used to be the end of life. The image of what "old" means is changing. For some, the older years are the fun years—years to travel, enjoy those things for which they have been saving. Some choose to remain active and involved; some choose to withdraw. Old age can take many directions and you have an important voice in how yours will be.

The quest for meaning often moves to the forefront in later years. The busy middle years often leave little time for reflection. Many of you were so busy bringing the bread home or caring for children you never took the time or perhaps had the inclination to wonder about life, to reflect on what is important. The first half of life is essentially about survival and adapting to change. The only constant at any stage of life is change. You are on a journey and always in process. Mid-life crises occur among those who believe that the momentum of life is always in a forward and upward direction—more relationships, more security, more money, more happiness. Few of us were properly prepared for the many obstacles in the road and had to learn the hard way that life is what happens to you on the journey. The trick is to enjoy the journey, moment by moment, instead of always anticipating "getting there." In a lecture, Joseph Campbell defined mid-life crisis as finally making it up the ladder of success only to discover the ladder is against the wrong building. *The Vintage Journey* helps you avoid "old age crisis" by asking you to pause and reflect on whether you are at the right building.

> *Be patient toward all that is unsolved in your heart*
> *and try to love the questions themselves. . . .*
> *The point is to love everything.*
> *Live the questions now.*
> —Rainer Maria Rilke, *Letters to a Young Poet*

> *People are different in fundamental ways.*
> *They want different things;*
> *they have different motives, purposes, aims,*
> *values, needs, drives, impulses, urges.*
> *Nothing is more fundamental than that.*
> *They believe differently; they think and behave differently.*
> —David Keirsey and Marilyn Bates, *Please Understand Me*

The questions that follow will help you recall your experiences and your learnings up to now. Sometimes all you need is an occasional open-ended sentence to get started.

- Tell me about . . .
- I was so excited when . . .
- If I could do one thing differently in my life, I would . . .
- If I could wish for one thing right now, mine would be . . .
- Life feels meaningful when . . .

This guide uses general, open-ended statements and questions like these but also includes more specific questions for contemplation. Look carefully through this section and check questions of particular interest to you or place an X on questions you'd rather skip. If you are a listener, read about how to listen effectively in appendix B. If you are taping the stories, read appendix A for tips.

It is your choice how deeply you want to delve into yourself, how vulnerable to let yourself be. You are the boss. Only you can make sense of your journey. In the first section leaf through the pages of questions and check the subjects that interest you most. You may choose to do one or two topics a session, or perhaps focus on one particular time period of your life. This book is your personal tool to help you uncover your embedded history and custom design your future. Welcome to your journey.

1 · *Integrating Your Yesterdays*

Reviewing your history provides an opportunity for personal integration. By retracing your experiences, you may develop a feeling for the rhythms of change in your life and a sense of what was important or inspirational. Remembering the good times is uplifting. Recalling how you struggled through times of difficulty expands your appreciation of your own resiliency. You are your own best teacher. You have witnessed the qualitative evolution of your own life. The questions in this chapter may help spark your integration process.

Birth

> **Date**
>
> **Time of day**
>
> **Place**
>
> **Your weight at birth**
>
> **What were you told about it?**

How old was your mother when you were born? Your father? Do you know how your name was chosen? Were you named after someone? Describe your very earliest memory. Do you remember your bedroom? Tell me about your hobbies. Pets. Friends. Clubs. Favorite possessions. Family holidays. What holiday was most fun? What were your Christmases like? Thanksgivings? Hanukkahs? Do you remember special birthday parties? Halloweens? Games you played? Other traditions? What sort of community did you grow up in? How did you fit in? What did you do for fun? Tell me some stories.

Did your family laugh a lot? Can you remember any particularly funny times? What parts did music, dance, art play in your life? Did you play any musical instruments? Were there any special talents you were known for? Who were your favorite relatives? Neighbors? Friends? Describe a smell or a sound that you associate with your childhood. What messages about life did you acquire from your childhood?

Family of Origin

When you visualize your parents, what do you see them doing? How are they dressed? Do you know how they met? What do you know about their ethnic background? Do you have pictures? What were your parents like? What did they do? What were they especially opinionated about? Did you share their opinions? Do you now?

How did they discipline you? How did your parents compliment you? Criticize you? How did you get along with your father? Mother? What advice did they give? What did they do for fun? Argue about? How did you make them happy? Were there any particular instances when you defied your family's expectations?

Now that you're older, how do you think your parents did? Do you consider your parents good role models? Why or why not? What skills did you learn from them? Who do you resemble? What traits do you get from your father? Your mother?

What didn't you ever ask your parents that you've always wanted to know? What was taboo in your household? What were the secrets? What weren't you supposed to question? Has there been any alcoholism or drug abuse in your family? How did your parents model "getting old"? Who has been the best model for you? Tell me about your parents.

What were some of the rules your family lived by?

What were some of your family sayings? For example: Winners never quit; quitters never win. Do as I say, not as I do. She's so wonderful; she never complains. Cleanliness is next to godliness. Brave boys don't cry. Anything worth doing is worth doing well.

Which of these messages did you believe at the time that you later chose to discard? What ones do you still agree with?

Tell me about your grandparents.

Tell me about your brother(s) and sisters(s).
Names   Birthdates

How did you get along with your sibling(s) as a youngster? Now? What was your birth rank?

How do you think your position in the family affected your life? What stories stick out in your mind?

Describe a favorite place where you have lived. Did you have a favorite spot in the house? Was it traumatic for you to leave home or were you glad to move on? What neighbors have been particularly memorable? Why?

Were there any family catastrophes that stick out in your memory? How did you deal with them? Did someone close to you die? How did you deal with the loss? Were there any periods of economic depression? How did you cope? Were there any natural disasters—flood, fire, hurricane, illness? What happened?

School

What is your educational history?
Elementary school_____graduated _____
Next school _____graduated _____
Next school _____graduated _____

Did you like school? What part? Why?
What stories do you remember?

Who were your most influential teachers? What did you like about them? With what figure in literature or mythology do you most identify? Why? What was your family's attitude toward education? What were your favorite subjects? Why? What did you do after school? What sports or activities were you involved in? If you had your schooling to do over again, what would you do differently? What advice do you have for others?

Work

What was your most rewarding job? Tell me about it.

The all-American question is, "What do you do?" What did you answer in the past? If you are retired, how do you answer now? Describe your first job? Were there promotions? Awards? Satisfactions?

If you did not work outside the home, was it a choice? How do you feel about it now?

What are your feelings about money?

How much importance have you placed on money?
___ enough importance
___ too much importance
___ about the right amount

What worries you most about your financial situation right now?

Did you work too hard, not hard enough, or about the right amount? Did/do you like your work? Who was your favorite boss? Least favorite? Do you prefer working alone or with others? Do you prefer working for yourself or for others? Do you have any regrets about choices not taken? Paths not pursued? How would you describe your earning power? Your financial status over the years? Now? Do you have any favorite work tale? Funny? Horrible? Unfair? Tell me about some of your proudest moments, your hardest decisions, your best decisions.

Have you served in the military? Where did you serve? What did you do? What impact did it have on you? How did you view military service then? Now?

Relationships

Who were your primary role models (family, clergy, teachers, sportspersons)? What did you admire about them?

Do you think that you have been a role model for anyone? Explain.

Who trusts you? How does that make you feel?

Who is your best friend now? What do you especially appreciate about him or her?

Do you have any dormant relationships that you want to revive? How will you do it?

Tell me about your marriage(s)/special relationship(s)? First date? How long a courtship? Other courtships? Tell me about your wedding. How did you know this was the person you wanted? What was the most romantic thing he or she ever did for you? What was the happiest time for the two of you? What qualities did you like best about her or him? Dislike? Did you tell this person these things? Can you now? What would you like to say?

How did your relationship(s) change over the years?

With whom have you laughed the most?

With whom have you cried?

Tell me about a major relationship in your life. Describe this person as if they were a character in a novel.

Those things that hurt, instruct.
—Benjamin Franklin

Rough Times

Before you begin this section, if parts of your life still feel too raw and painful, skip them for now. You are your own best guide. Go on to another part of your life for the time being. No need to force it. If you have already grieved an old loss and moved on, let it be.

What was the hardest time in your life? Were there several? Scariest times? What deaths have had the biggest impact on you? Have you been with someone when he or she died? Did you ever have any money stolen from you or your house robbed? Describe the feelings. How else have people taken advantage of you?

How did you cope?

What were some of your loneliest periods? How did you get through them?

All families have problems. What were some of yours?

	Not a problem	Somewhat stressful	Very stressful
Money problems due to illness/hardship			
Money problems due to loss of income			
Money problems due to inability to budget			
Marital conflicts			
Infidelities			
Job conflicts			
Significant losses			
Alcohol or drug abuse			
Physical, sexual, or emotional abuse			
Frequent moves			
Psychological problems			
Trouble with the law			
Deaths			

What did you learn because of these hardships?

Who is it easiest for you to lean on? Who do you feel comfortable asking for assistance? Why?

What was your most physically painful experience? Broken bones? Operations?

What was the most emotionally painful time? How did you survive it?

What are you grieving now? Losses need to be grieved. (See part 3 for suggestions.) It is a lonely and also a necessary time. No one can do your grieving for you. You grieve in your own unique style, which can vary from one loss to another. You must feel your loss and your grief before you can move on.

Feel no pressure to share events. You know best whether sharing might bring some peace to you. Just be aware that both the tragedies and the triumphs are part of the whole you. Recognize the importance and extent of these events; most of all, give yourself credit for coping and surviving.

Let in the feelings;
let out the feelings.
You cannot move on unless you feel.

We all have gloomy places and we learn that we must walk through them, not around them to get to the light again. Incredibly sad things happen. You feel sad because you have cared and caring again is, ironically, what helps you recover.

A friend is someone who knows
The song in your heart and
Plays back the words to you
When you forget how they go.
—Author Unknown

Happy Times

What was the happiest period in your life? Why?

When did you feel the best about yourself? Why?

Do you have a favorite place?

With whom have you had a wonderful relationship? Why is/was it special?

Memorable Stories

Think of some great places of beauty where you've been. What's the greatest adventure you've been on? What did you learn about yourself? Name some favorite pastimes, movies, radio shows, sayings, scary events, buddies, true friends. What incidents do you recall that gave you a sense of fulfillment? As a child, what did you want to be when you grew up? Who were your best friends? Did you have a gang? What were your favorite pets? What were your favorite stories about them? Do you have a pet or want one now? What home remedies do you recall? Do you still use them? What home remedies did you create? What were your favorite foods then? Now? What recipes did you inherit? What recipes are you passing on to your children? To others? Did you have any special victories? Triumphs? Humiliations?

Major Events

Where were you when Kennedy was shot? Pearl Harbor was attacked? Roosevelt died? Normandy was invaded? The stock market crashed? The zeppelin *Hindenburg* burned? Martin Luther King, Jr., was assassinated? Your parent died? U.S. astronaut Neil Armstrong walked on the moon? The space shuttle *Challenger* blew up? Natural disasters struck (hurricanes, tornadoes, fires, floods)? What do you remember? How did you feel?

How were you affected by the Great Depression? Prohibition? World War I? World War II? Korea? Vietnam? Technological advances? Do you remember any air raids? Did you have a Victory Garden?

Did you ever work for any social causes? What did you do?

How many presidents have there been in your lifetime? Who was your favorite? Who have been some of the inspiring leaders? What did you admire about them?

Car Stories

Did you take any family car trips? What was the fanciest, most expensive car you've owned? Ever seen? If you could have any kind of car you want, what would you choose? Were you ever involved in any accidents? Tell about terrible drivers you've known.

Travel

What great trips have you taken? Where? Who is your favorite traveling companion? What places are on your to-be-visited list?

Eating

What are some of your all-time favorite foods? Do you recall any spectacular eating orgy? What's the best party you ever gave? Attended? What are your favorite restaurants? Who is the best cook you've ever known? Worst cook? What are your favorite recipes? Who do you associate with them? Have your tastes changed? What do you have a craving for right now?

Gifts

What was the best gift you ever received? What was the best gift you ever gave? If you could have anything, what would it be? Fantasy? In reality?

Sports

Who is your all-time favorite hero? What are the best games you've ever seen? What sport did you have the most fun participating in? What are your honors or achievements? What was your biggest disappointment?

Clothes

Do you tend to be conservative or flashy? If you went some place where no one knew you, what kind of clothing might you wear? What's your favorite kind of outfit? What was your fanciest dress-up outing? How have fashions changed? Do you remember a particularly foolish clothing purchase?

Firsts

What is your earliest memory of all?

Do you remember the first time you saw a television? When? What early programs do you remember?

Do you remember your first plane or train ride? How many modes of transportation have you used?

What was your first major hurt? Sadness?

When did you first see the ocean? Swim in it? Water-ski?

What was your first experience earning money? How much did you earn?

When was the first time you felt "on your own" or lived alone?

Who was your first boyfriend or girlfriend? When was your first kiss?

What do you remember about the first time you made love?

Holidays

What are your Christmas/Hanukkah traditions? New Year's Eve? Halloween? Thanksgiving? Easter? Passover? What did/do you do? What did you eat?

2 · Who Am I Right Now?

Your stories and experiences of the past are part of who you are today. This chapter gives you the opportunity to describe yourself as you see yourself now. You know yourself better than anyone else possibly can.

Describe Yourself

Circle five adjectives that best describe you:
happy, content, bored, tired, enthusiastic, achy, apathetic, rigid, old, patriotic, sensitive, lucky, opinionated, indecisive, resourceful, caring, introverted, extroverted, sentimental, stubborn, easy-going, sick, healthy, loving, fulfilled, sad, boring, religious, wise, learning, active, humbled, interesting, cheerful, complaining, lonely, grouchy, busy, sexy, cynical, nasty, depressed, productive, poor, well-off, satisfied, searching, funny, growing, regretful, interested, free, patient, impatient, jealous, angry, other _____
Talk about the five adjectives you chose in more detail.

Are they mostly positive or negative?

What adjectives would others choose to describe you?

What term best describes what you consider your essence to be?

How many people know the "real" you?

What do you like most about yourself?

What don't you like about yourself? How can you change it?

> *Life can only be understood backwards,*
> *but it must be lived forwards.*

Lifeline Exercise

In a "lifeline" exercise, you are asked to draw a line with your birthdate at one end and your projected death date at the other. This gives you a visual perspective of the rhythm and flow of your life.

Years   0   10   20   30   40   50   60   70   80   90   100

Birth date _____ Death date

Draw a line zigzagging the lifeline that indicates the "good" years (above the lifeline) versus the "not-so-good" years (below the lifeline). In each decade, what was your primary role (student, wage-earner, parent)? What is it now? What were your turning points? Who was the biggest influence in your life in each decade? Major losses? Was there a major move? New home? Job? Major illness? Accident? Financial setbacks? How did you feel about these events? How did you cope? Was there a special person in your life who befriended you, became a mentor at some certain period of your life? How did he or she make a difference for you?

Feelings

How do you celebrate? Express joy? Happiness?

How does your family deal with hard times, negative feelings?

__   Try to act as if nothing is happening.

__   If not possible, discuss issue calmly and openly.

__   Cry, emote, talk about situation.

__   Divert with humor.

__   Yell and swear at each other.

__   Some sulk, others stalk out.

__   Violence erupts.

Describe how you deal with anger.

What irritates you? Makes you nervous? Squeamish?

When have you lost your temper?

When have you expressed your anger in a way that makes you proud?

What experiences have taught you the most?

When something doesn't go the way you want it to, what would you most likely tell yourself? Check as many as you wish.

___ It is my (spouse, boss, the economy's) fault.

___ It was my fault.

___ Next time, I will do . . . differently.

Have you ever taken a stand for or about something that made you unpopular with your family and/or friends?

Who has discussed his or her relationship with you most directly and honestly? How does that make you feel?

What does intimacy mean to you? How important is intimacy in your life?

How comfortable are you about expressing negative feelings? Intimate, positive feelings?

How do you rate your ability to listen (circle one)?   excellent
okay
poor

Are you experiencing resistance or tension in your life right now? What is it about? What would you have to do to let go of it (see part 3, "Letting Go, Forgiveness")?

What makes you happy/satisfied now?

Stress

The part of your life that stresses you the most is: job, finances, health, relationships, school, the world (or community), or everything? Say more about this.

How does your body respond to feelings of anxiety?

Identify a time when you felt at peace, calm, happy. What made it that way?

What would you do if you knew you could not fail?

Religion/Spirituality

Tell me about your religion/spirituality and its role in your life? How do you practice/celebrate it?

Do you believe in God? What is your image of God? Do you believe in a Higher Power? Has this changed for you over the years? Do you feel connected to all others? To nature? What was your religious background? How active were you in church/synagogue? How important was religion in your life then? Describe a typical Sabbath day as a child. Do you remember a particularly meaningful childhood experience? Did you fear death as a child? Do you fear it now? Do your beliefs help you deal with any fears you might have? How important is it to you that others think the way you do? If you have children, do they share your faith? Who/what influenced you the most in your spiritual journey? What makes you feel connected to all others? What about your religion/spirituality helps you the most?

Interests

What subjects do you feel passionately about? Possibilities may include greed, dishonesty, faithlessness, gun control, inaccessibility of health care, homelessness, abortion, premarital sex, extramarital sex, euthanasia, unfair taxes, pornography, falsehoods, suicide, test tube babies, nuclear waste, exploitation of the environment, violence on the streets, tense racial/ethnic relations, others? Discuss.

What messages did you get from your family about the importance of appearance? Family? Money? Marriage? Patriotism? Church or synagogue? College? Grades in school? Career?   Cleanliness? Diet? Environment? Discuss how you have changed over time.

Are your political views similar or dissimilar to those of your parents?

Relationships

Family

Please expand your definition of family to fit for you. It does not have to be family by marriage or blood relationship. The American Home Economics Association defines family as two or more persons who have commitments to one another over a period of time and share resources, responsibility for decisions, and values and goals.

For those who have children, tell me about them.
Names   Birthdays

Where do they live now?

If you are divorced or widowed, how old were your children when that happened?

When did each child leave home? For what reason?

Did you enjoy parenting most of the time, some of the time, or not too much?

Did you find parenting more enjoyable when the kids were very young, during their teen years, when they were young adults, when they became adults, or all of the time?

What has been most rewarding to you as a parent?

Which of your children is most like you now?

Who best understands the way you think and feel?

Who is most unlike you?

Who is the most responsible?

Who would you prefer to make decisions for you if you were unable?

Was there much sibling rivalry among your children? If so, why (jealousy, competitiveness, turf battles)?

What were some of your toughest times as a parent? How did you handle them? What did you learn?

When you have contact with your children now, who does the initiating (you, your child, both)?

In what ways are you proud of your children?

What do you like the most about your relationships with your children? Grandchildren? Great-grandchildren?

What would you like to be different about those relationships?

In what way do you think that you model "getting old" for younger people that might influence them most positively? Negatively?

How much inclusion in your children's lives do you want?

___ a great deal
___ some
___ not much

Do you want to know about your children's:

	Yes	No
marital happiness?	___	___
relationships?	___	___
problems with their children?	___	___
successes?	___	___
jobs, financial problems?	___	___
jobs, financial successes?	___	___
adventures, trips?	___	___

Would you say that your family was:
___ sincerely affectionate towards one another

___ moderately affectionate

___ not good at displaying affection but you felt loved

___ not good at displaying affection because it wasn't there

Do you talk with your family about your: **Often enough**   **Not enough**

	Often enough	Not enough
feelings	___	___
differences of opinion	___	___
fears	___	___
projects, interests	___	___
opinions about current events	___	___
opinions about pending decisions	___	___
finances	___	___
health	___	___
future plans	___	___
feelings for them	___	___

Are there things you regret doing or avoid discussing that you can discuss now and perhaps make amends? It is important to acknowledge any of these events, apologize, and forgive yourself or the others involved. Acknowledge what you have learned and would perhaps do differently, and then let it go. (Information on how to do this is detailed in part 3.)

Friends

Who has been your friend the longest? What have you been through together?

Do you have different friends for different needs? Hunting? Fishing? Shopping? Eating? Having fun? Philosophizing? Who are they?

Who do you go to if you want to be listened to and understood?

Do you prefer to be alone or with others? Describe. Is it easy for you to get close to another? What kind of friends do you choose? Do you share your feelings with your friend(s)? Do you hug/show affection with your friend(s)? Has this changed over time? Do you feel listened to, understood? What would you like "more of" from a friend? When have you known that you were being a good friend to someone? A good friend to yourself?

Retirement

How do you feel about retirement? How did you view it at age 40? Age 60? Now?

What advice do you have about planning for retirement?

What do you now have time for that you didn't before?

Who do you want to see more of?

Were you reluctant or eager to retire? What were/are major adjustments? What are you excited about doing? How can you now use the abilities you have acquired?

A Typical Day

Describe a typical day in your life right now.

How much time do you have alone?

  ___ too much

  ___ not enough

  ___ just about right

To whom do you typically talk?

What's your favorite part of the day?

Has this changed over the years?

Home/Community

What does "home" signify to you?

What do you like best about where you live now? Are/were you active in your community? How?

What are some material things you own that are important to you? Tell me about them.

Leisure Time

What are some of the ways you use your leisure time?

What are some examples of your favorite songs? Music? Television programs? Radio shows? Kinds of dancing and with whom? Movies? Movie stars? Books? Authors? Art?

Are you satisfied with how you spend your time? What can you do about it? What do you enjoy most? Why? How has this changed over the years? What did you used to like to do? Are you competitive?

How is/was this expressed? Do you have daily chores? What chores have you had other times in your life that stick out in your mind?

Time Chart

How much time do you spend	Not Enough	Enough	Too Much
Alone			
With people you care about			
With people you don't like			
On spiritual endeavors—praying, meditating			
Volunteering, helping others			
Working for pay			
Reading			
Watching television			
Listening to music/radio			
Going to church/synagogue			
Caregiving (spouse, parents, friends, baby-sitting)			
Shopping/errands			
Doing activities of daily living			
Walking/hiking			
Gardening			
Fishing/hunting			
Watching birds			
Traveling			
Exercising			
Other			

What can you do to change the "not enough" to "enough"?

Oppression

Oppression is about being confined, restricted, or discriminated against by individuals or societal structures solely because you belong to a particular group or category of people. In the United States, this happens to some degree to all, although less so for young, educated, able-bodied, white, Christian, heterosexual males. If you are part of an oppressed group because of age, race, gender, disability, religion, or sexual orientation, consider these questions. What particular experiences of personal exclusion or prejudice come to mind? If you experienced oppression as a child, how did this affect you? If you have retired, do you ever feel like people treat you as if you're less important? How does it make you feel? Have you ever been sexually harassed? What were some of your most hurtful experiences? How were you supported? What are your feelings about any oppression you have experienced?

What have you learned?

What advice do you have?

Fantasy Questions

If you could have anything you wanted, what would you ask for?

If you had a month or six weeks to live and an unlimited budget, what would you do?

What one personal possession would you like to keep if you had to choose?

Humor

Who is the funniest person you know? Say something about him or her.

Who do you know who has the best laugh?

Name three things you had fun doing as a child.

What do you enjoy about watching children?

When was the last time you had a good laugh? What about?

Is your sense of humor, your spirit, more activated around certain people? Who?

Help your memory. Write down your favorite jokes and funniest memories so you will have them handy when you need to be pepped up. When you are telling your story, you will no doubt come across some priceless ones.

You don't stop laughing because you grow old;
you grow old because you stop laughing.
—John Bratner

My Humor Journal

Conclusion

Part 1, "This Is Who I Am," gives you a framework for reviewing your life. It also grants you permission to indulge yourself in some valuable introspection that will help you discover what relationships and experiences have shaped you and what you truly value. Notice the many roles you have had, all the things you have done, all the losses you have survived. You are made up of these things.

Now you can focus on the parts of you that you want, and create your best possible future. Taking this time to get reacquainted with yourself is a magnificent gift that only you can give yourself. If you share your story and your insights with another, the process of discovery can be doubly rewarding. Your experiences then become an important legacy, a bridge to immortality. Perhaps this time spent looking at your past and within yourself will help you to affirm your life, see how the parts fit into the whole, and will bring clarity to what is most life-giving and important to you. Soak up your beautiful and thought-provoking stories, revel in your good memories, appreciate your ability to learn and make hard decisions, and marvel at life's complexities and mystery. Your many years of living give you a fresh perspective unavailable to you when you were younger. Celebrate your journey!

Evening unravels the secret,
webbed in mystery by the day.

This is who I am!

Part 2 This Is My Responsibility

This is a revolutionary time. There is an explosion in the number of persons living into their seventies, eighties, and nineties and they are discovering more and more creative ways to use this period of their lives. They are generally healthy and vigorous. One-third of those over the age of eighty-five report no health limitations, and another third report only minor limitations. It is hard to generalize about the characteristics of this older age group. One seventy-five-year-old may be confined to a wheelchair, while another the same age plays golf. While one ninety-year-old may be quite content and fulfilled, another feels sad and empty. Members of this age group are more dissimilar than any other because they have been shaped by so many different variables and experiences.

There are only a few models, few guideposts, and no generic recipe for living life fully. However, there may be consensus that the number one ingredient for the recipe is the need for choice. People of any age need to feel that they have choices and some sense of control over their lives.

A successful age is about thriving, not just surviving.
—Robert Butler, *Aging and Mental Health*

The best way to thrive is to take responsibility for your life, to make choices, to be your own self-manager. This section will help you sort through what is important to you, lay the necessary groundwork for responsible planning, and encourage you to do it. There are many ways that you can plan for this time of life but the fundamentals are relatively constant. First, you need to obtain the most current information available on your subjects of interest. Second, you need to clarify what your feelings and values are and make choices that are congruent with them. Third, you need to communicate that awareness informally to those close to you and formally in ways that further guarantee your wishes will be carried out.

The questions and values clarification exercises, along with the valuable information supplied in this section, allow you to add to your evolving picture of the "whole" you and what "quality of life" means to you. This thorough and expansive approach guides you toward responsible decision-making about your later years by discussing housing options, services available, and financial and property planning, focusing primarily on health care and after-death planning. The information about yourself gleaned from part 1, "This Is Who I Am," and from the quality of life and values clarification exercises in this section will give you the self-knowledge to enable you take charge of planning and preparing for your best possible old age. The appendix includes advance directive forms for a living will and durable power of attorney, along with a glossary of terms. This section provides enough background material to help you actually complete these forms if you wish. People feel best about themselves when they know that they have some choices and that they have responsibly "put things in order."

3 · *Values Clarification*

Prioritize Your Values

It is important for people to know how strongly they feel about things. All too often, health-care professionals or even family members assume they know what someone else wants, an assumption that might be entirely wrong. Some people believe that a clean house and a clean body are paramount. Others could not care less. Some like to have people around and are generally sociable, while others prefer to be alone or with a select few. Some people enjoy a routine time to get up, go to bed, get the mail, and watch certain television shows. Others prefer a more random, unstructured life. Some are indoors people, while others thrive outside.

It is important to become aware of what is important to you and to verbalize this. If you eventually reside in a nursing home—20 percent of Americans will at some point after the age of eighty—and the most important thing to you is breathing fresh air and getting outside to watch the birds and squirrels, think about that now so you can plan and let people know. Health-care professionals do follow care plans. Left to their own decision-making, they may assume that being clean and fed is most important. Perhaps it is not most important to you, however. Let people in charge know what you value and what being treated in a dignified manner means for you and ask that it be written into your care plan and respected.

Our society has a sad way of viewing the very old or sick in terms of whatever ailment or symptom they have. You become identified as the person with Alzheimer's, the poor dear with arthritis, or the person who behaves badly. Seemingly gone is the person who has a high appreciation for music or fine food, who loves people, who loved fun and only secondarily has one or more of the above limitations. This is your opportunity to make it perfectly clear who you are—the whole you, what you've done, what you like to do, and what your values are—so that you will not be looked at solely in terms of your "functional deficits." Functional deficits become the language of the frail. This is bad business because, when other people start defining you that way, you may soon start identifying with that definition yourself.

What one person perceives to be a behavior problem could actually be a strength. Child psychologists have long recognized that the child in a dysfunctional family who "acts out" is often the healthiest one in the family system, the one who is trying to break out. A stubborn elder may be the one who has the courage to defy the system, which is what actually has the functional deficit.

Identify those things in your life that are important to you. Here are some questions for reflection and discussion:

- Which is more important to you, having someone to talk to or having a clean house? (You can like both!)
- Which is more important to you, having your hair done or walking in the woods?
- What type of music do you prefer?
- If your state of health becomes shaky, would you rather remain alone in your home with the attendant risks or hire someone to be with you?
- Would you rather visit with one person at a time or do you prefer to be with people in groups or a party atmosphere?
- If you were to move to a nursing home facility, would you prefer one with particular ethnic or religious ties or one with no particular affiliation?

Your responses don't have to be either/or, but if you have strong feelings, it is important to say so. Unless you tell people what you want, you can't expect to get it. You don't necessarily always get what you want even when you ask, but your chances are greatly improved. So often older people with whom I work believe they are misunderstood. On further inquiry I discover that they are misunderstood for good reason. For example, when their adult children ask how they are doing, they reply, "Just fine," because they value not complaining. They paint themselves into a corner because their pride prevents them from being honest with those people who care. Saying exactly what you want is so basic, yet it is a primary communication problem. Don't assume that people can tell how you are. You can be fine most of the time and still need help some of the time. You simply can't expect others to know what you need if you don't explicitly tell them what help you'd appreciate getting from them. Learning how to ask for what you want and to "receive well" may be one of your hardest life lessons and one of the most important behaviors to model. Think carefully about those things you value highly. What are they?

This exercise asks you to prioritize traditional values. Rank the following eighteen values in order of importance to you. They may all be important but it is the relative importance that is significant.

____ Salvation (eternal life)

____ Happiness (pleasure)

____ Global peace

____ Self-respect

____ Social recognition

____ A comfortable life

____ Stimulation

____ Wisdom

____ Inner harmony

____ Independence (freedom to choose)

____ Excitement

____ Health

____ Serenity

____ Sexual intimacy

____ A sense of accomplishment

____ Equal opportunity

____ Freedom from pain

____ Preservation of the environment

____ Other _____

Have Your Values Changed?

Values change with the times, your knowledge, your experience, and societal influence. How have your feelings about these subjects changed over time?

	Then	Now
Appropriate age to marry	_____	_____
Appropriate age to have children	_____	_____
Premarital sex	_____	_____
Divorce	_____	_____
Working mothers	_____	_____
Saving money	_____	_____
Work before play	_____	_____
Expression of:		
Anger	_____	_____
Love	_____	_____
Touch/hugging	_____	_____
Guilt	_____	_____
Fear	_____	_____
Success	_____	_____
Asking for what you want	_____	_____
Respect for elders	_____	_____
Meaning of health	_____	_____
Meaning of "old"	_____	_____
War/patriotism	_____	_____
Politics	_____	_____
Trust of public officials	_____	_____
Fear for safety	_____	_____
Alcohol	_____	_____
Diet	_____	_____
Risk-taking	_____	_____
Meaning of beauty	_____	_____
Funerals	_____	_____
Cremation	_____	_____
Homosexuality	_____	_____
Environmental awareness	_____	_____

The previous exercise points out the necessity of continuing to discuss with those close to you how you feel about issues and what is important to you. Notice how you are exhibiting movement, always in process. Some values remain constant; others change over time.

It is also illuminating to examine how strongly you feel about some issues. The next exercise will help clarify this.

Where Is Your Line?

Which of the following situations do you consider to be a serious ethical breach? (On a scale of 1-7, 1 = no problem and 7 = serious problem.) Circle what fits for you.

Smoking marijuana	1 2 3 4 5 6 7
Premarital sex	1 2 3 4 5 6 7
Extramarital sex	1 2 3 4 5 6 7
Breaking a promise	1 2 3 4 5 6 7
Using cocaine	1 2 3 4 5 6 7
Drinking to excess	1 2 3 4 5 6 7
Euthanasia	1 2 3 4 5 6 7
Suicide	1 2 3 4 5 6 7
Assisted suicide	1 2 3 4 5 6 7
Taking pencils, paper clips from office	1 2 3 4 5 6 7
Taking typewriters, computer, software	1 2 3 4 5 6 7
Falsely calling in sick	1 2 3 4 5 6 7
Making personal calls on office phone	1 2 3 4 5 6 7
Padding expense accounts	1 2 3 4 5 6 7
False advertising	1 2 3 4 5 6 7
Lying	1 2 3 4 5 6 7
Lying to avoid hurting someone	1 2 3 4 5 6 7
Trespassing	1 2 3 4 5 6 7
Jaywalking	1 2 3 4 5 6 7

Fudging on income tax return		1 2 3 4 5 6 7
Capital punishment		1 2 3 4 5 6 7
Abortion		1 2 3 4 5 6 7

Part of your uniqueness is that you draw the line at a different point from others. It doesn't necessarily make you right or wrong, just different.

Locus of Control Quiz

Locus of control is a construct that indicates the amount of control you expect to have in your life. Persons who want as much information as possible and expect a high degree of input in order to feel content with decisions have a high internal locus of control. Persons who do not desire control and in fact experience a higher degree of anxiety if forced to make a decision exhibit an external locus of control. After reading the following statements, circle the number that describes the degree to which you agree or disagree with each one:

1	2	3	4	5
Strongly agree		Neutral		Strongly disagree

1. I feel that I have a lot of choice in who my friends are.   1 2 3 4 5
2. I expect to be involved in health care decisions concerning
   my own health.   1 2 3 4 5
3. When I have been presented with a crisis in the past I have
   done pretty well with solving or adapting to it.   1 2 3 4 5
4. I have very strong opinions.   1 2 3 4 5
5. I trust my own decisions when I make them.   1 2 3 4 5

Total Score _____

Scoring: High internal locus of control: 5-10
High external locus of control: 20-25

If you have a high external locus of control, you may or may not want to participate in the exercises in the remaining part of the book, but, if this is the case, it then becomes even more important to give careful thought to whom you trust when you designate a surrogate decision-maker for health-care decisions.

Quality of Life

What do you enjoy doing?

What percentage of your time do you spend doing things you enjoy?

What makes you feel good about yourself?

How would you define "quality time"?

D. Doyle, G. W. C. Hanks, and N. MacDonald define quality of life as "the relationship between an individual's expectations and the reality of the situation." Perception of what reality is changes with the introduction of new events, new opportunities and interests, and losses of different magnitude. Your expectations change as well, so the notion of quality of life is not static. It is endlessly changing and constantly varying as you accumulate experiences.

What Makes Quality for You?

	Enough?	Want More?	Want Less?
Relationship with God (Jesus, Higher Power, Inner Wisdom, etc.)			
Someone who listens to your:			
feelings			
needs			
preferences			
reminiscences			
Someone with whom to laugh			
Someone who gives:			
warmth			
touch			
companionship			
sexual pleasure			
intellectual stimulation			
Others for whom to care			
Freedom to Make decisions for yourself			
Be alone; have privacy			
Travel			
Get out in nature			
Engage in pleasurable activities			
Work for social change			
Engage in creative activities			

What can you change to generate more quality for yourself?

Values Reflection

At some period of your life you will probably have to make some hard decisions about your living and health-care arrangements. For instance, 70 percent of the population will have to make some sort of life-support decision at the very end of life. This segment of the book asks questions and paints scenarios to help you figure out how you think and feel about these issues and why you respond the way you do. This kind of reflection can be difficult, but please persevere because it is exactly these delicate areas of discussion, which can be so easily avoided, that can give you and whomever you are sharing your thoughts with the insights needed to make the most fitting decisions for your future well-being.

Reflect on the Following

You have a chronic illness and have been growing more dependent on your child or spouse for care for years. You want to remain at home, but your caregiver is getting worn out. Do you think that your caregiver should have as much to say as you do, if not more, about your care plan?

If your adult child asked you to come live with him or her and you felt that it was time to make some sort of a move, would you:

- A. accept
- B. refuse; stay put
- C. refuse; seek another option

When you are old, single and frail, would you prefer to:

- A. live alone in your own home or apartment, recognizing the risks and freedoms?
- B. live with family?
- C. live in own apartment/condo with people of all ages?
- D. live in apartment complex for seniors only (amenities available such as transportation, optional meals, activities)?
- E. It depends

"It depends" is a common and understandable first response to many questions. The only way to ascertain what "It depends" means is to uncover as much information as possible about the variables involved in the situation. Your life review—the discussion around specific "what if" dilemmas—generates the information needed to discover what "it depends" means. When you know and have expressed your feelings and biases about health care, preferred living arrangements, financial options, and personal preferences, the fog begins to clear. Some people worry about their old age. Others don't. Even the nonworriers wonder at times, "If something happens to me, what will happen to him or her?" or "I'm shoveling the snow and mowing the grass now, but I suppose some day I won't be able to . . . What then?" Most want to be in charge of making their own arrangements but unfortunately some combination of procrastination and denial too often prevail. While things are going well, you put off planning. The best planning occurs when you have time and aren't in crisis.

What's most important to you? Perhaps you love tinkering around your home doing chores. Perhaps you love your neighborhood and knowing people when you go shopping at the grocery store. Perhaps you no longer feel up to the maintenance your house requires and you're finding that you get out less and less and are seeing fewer people. There is quite a large group of older adults who continue living in their lifetime houses who become socially isolated and miserably lonely. Others disengage socially and love it. Since it is impossible to generalize, it is important to inventory what you like.

If you required considerable assistance in activities of daily living (feeding, toileting, bathing, and dressing), would you prefer:

    A.   remaining in your own home with:
        1. family assistance
        2. professional homecare service

    B.   moving to apartment with:
        1. family assistance
        2. professional home-care service

    C.   moving in with family member who would then become your caregiver

    D.   moving to a facility that provides more care

Your neighbor, Lucy, is eighty-two years old and lives alone in a single family dwelling in a rather unneighborly suburban area. She is mildly demented and occasionally wanders out of the house and gets lost, but she has not been injured to date. Her doctor and home-health nurse feel that Lucy should move to a nursing home, but Lucy refuses to do that and her daughter who lives in another state doesn't want to get involved. Since Lucy insists on staying at home, the home-health nurse wants to provide two hours of home-health aide service seven days a week, but Lucy will accept services only two days a week because she thinks she is "doing fine, thank you." You feel responsible and worried about her. What should you do? Why do you respond this way?

Roy is eighty-five years old and lives with his daughter who works out of the home five days a week. He is extremely frail and needs help with many things such as walking, bathing, and meal preparation. Roy has episodes of confusion, but his physician has not been able to diagnose any dementia. On the days that his daughter works, she leaves her father alone in the locked house for about four hours until the home-health aide arrives; the aide then stays with Roy until the daughter returns. The daughter has refused more home-health aide service because she says she can't afford it. Her father says that he doesn't mind staying home alone. To date, he has not been injured while staying alone.

What do you think about this? How would you like it to be handled if you were Roy?

Two years ago Stephan, seventy-one, underwent a colostomy for colon cancer and then underwent x-ray therapy when the cancer recurred. Now blood tests suggest that the cancer has spread to the liver. While often drowsy, Stephan has nevertheless communicated to various persons, including his nephew, that he realizes he is approaching the end of his life, is tired of medical procedures, and wishes they would "just leave me alone." He has verbalized his feelings but has written no advance directive, believing he should not have to fill out any legal paraphernalia. The nephew hears that the surgeon plans to treat Stephan aggressively with radiation and surgical procedures in spite of his protests to the contrary.

The surgeon admits that Stephan is terminally ill, that cure is impossible, and that death will occur within months even with aggressive therapy. Still, he argues, "If we take it upon ourselves to end his life before then, we are playing God. Who gave us that right? And how would we feel if the week after he died, somebody discovered the cure for cancer? And how do we know that Stephan is in his right mind anyhow? I've been brought up to believe that human life is sacred, and we ought to do anything possible to preserve it." Do you agree with the doctor? What would you do if you were the nephew?

Jane has an eighty-eight-year-old friend, Alice, about whom she is worried. She really cares about Alice and doesn't know what to do. Alice has a lot of spirit and has taught Jane much about being tough and persevering. Alice is hard headed about some things, but Jane admires how she plugs along. Lately, Alice has grown weak and dizzy. Last week, Jane noticed a gash on Alice's forehead and Alice confided that she had fallen. She refuses to go to doctors and above all doesn't want her daughter, Shirley, to know how weak she is. Alice tells Shirley all sorts of untruths over the phone about all she does and how well she is.

Jane is caught in a confidentiality muddle. Alice asks her, with a twinkle in her eye but with obvious conviction, "not to let the cat out of the bag" and tell her daughter about her recent difficulties. Alice says that she "doesn't want anyone to worry." Jane is beginning to feel irresponsible because she thinks that she is the only one Alice trusts and that something ought to be done. Do you think Jane should tell Shirley how Alice is really doing? What other options might there be?

This morning, Elizabeth's daughter telephoned her and said, "Mother, I'd like to have you move in with me now. I have an extra room for you, and you know it would be the best thing for you to do. I understand you are having trouble taking care of things by yourself, and I don't want you going to a nursing home." Elizabeth had been expecting her daughter to tell her this for some time, but now that it has happened, she doesn't know what to do. She appreciates her daughter's concern and willingness to help, but she isn't sure she really wants to live with her. She has heard about a new residential home in her area, and several of her friends and acquaintances have moved there and seem to like it very much. The home is for people who are still active and not physically disabled, and it has an activity program for the residents, which sounds good to Elizabeth.

Elizabeth knows her daughter is very much opposed to homes for older people, and she can recall her daughter saying several years ago that there would always be a place for Elizabeth in her home when the time came that Elizabeth could no longer look after herself. However, now that her daughter has called and asked her to come, she is troubled and uncertain and wonders whether to accept her daughter's offer or try the residential home instead. What do you think you would do if you were Elizabeth? What would be the pros and cons of living with a son or daughter? What would be the pros and cons of living in a facility especially for seniors? What kind of a facility can you envision for yourself?

You promised your parent (or spouse) that you would never put him or her in a nursing home, but, after years of caregiving to the best of your ability, you think that you must do so. Would you break your promise? Discuss.

You are forty-five years old and have been offered a good business opportunity in a distant city. Your elderly mother doesn't want you to move because she is getting more dependent on your help and affection. She rejects the idea of moving with you. Would you move? Discuss.

The proper dose of pain medication is the dose that is sufficient to relieve pain even to the point of unconsciousness. Do you agree or disagree with this statement? Discuss.

By consensus of the American Medical Society and American Academy of Neurology, people in a persistent vegetative state (PVS) feel no pain and have no awareness. Some people are troubled by allowing these people to be taken off life-support devices. If you were in a state of permanent unconsciousness (PVS), would you want to be maintained by artificial measures?

If you disagree with the stated wishes of your parent or your spouse, would you make health-care and quality of life decisions according to his or her values rather than yours if he or she became unable to make decisions?

Do you think decisions about type of funeral or whether or not to be cremated should be up to the surviving family or to the previously stated wishes of the deceased?

Your father is eighty years old. You are worried about his driving. Even though he tries to be cautious, his vision is failing. He ricochets off curbs and has particular trouble with his nighttime driving because of the glare. You love him and know that he will be hurt and defensive if you bring up the subject. Would you:

     a. do nothing and pray for a minor accident in which no one would be hurt so that the police or Department of Motor Vehicles would become involved and you would not be forced to take action?

     b. carefully bring up the subject, stating your concern, then back off, hoping he would take some action?

     c. state your concerns and insist on some action.

Your father continues to drive. You and others make excuses to avoid riding with him—for your own safety. You worry about the safety of others. Would you:

    a. still do nothing?

    b. bring up the subject again and request that he see his physician for an assessment of his visual acuity and a judgment about his potential driving competence?

    c. remove an important part from the motor so that it mysteriously won't start?

    d. hide the keys?

    e. tell him you are going to notify the Department of Motor Vehicles requesting an intervention—a mandatory vision test, written/road test?

    f. notify the Department of Motor Vehicles but not tell your father?

This is a very delicate issue in most families. What do you think should be done? Would you respond differently if he were forty years old instead of eighty? Do you think if someone ignores or is unaware of decreasing ability to drive safely it is the moral responsibility of the family to act in some way? If you were having trouble with the glare at night while driving, what would you do? If you began to have "close calls" and felt that your driving reactions were slipping, what would you do?

If your doctor determines that you have the early symptoms of Alzheimer's, do you want to be told?

Some drugs that relieve pain reduce cognitive functioning. Would you choose to have pain rather than experience a reduction in lucidity?

> A. Yes, if moderated pain.
>
> B. No, if moderate pain.
>
> C. Yes, if extreme, intractable pain.
>
> D. No, want to be lucid.

If your doctor determines that you have a terminal illness and your death is imminent, would you want to be told?

Should heart/liver transplants be available only for those who can afford them? Do you think your age should be a consideration when deciding about expensive transplant operations? Should the government pay for these operations?

A proxy decision-maker decided to try a ventilator for awhile on a permanently comatose family member just in case some miracle happened. Seeing no change nor hope of recovery, the decision-maker requested its withdrawal. Do you think the ventilator should be withdrawn? Do you consider withdrawal from the ventilator:

a. just another hard decision—no different than starting treatment?

b. a more difficult decision because you would probably be allowing a person to die?

c. murder?

In the same scenario, if the treatment were artificial tube feeding and hydration, would you consider the proxy decision-maker's request for withdrawal

a. just another hard decision—no different than starting treatment?

b. a more difficult decision because you would probably be allowing a person to die?

c. murder?

Do you consider artificial tube feeding and hydration a medical procedure that is optional—sometimes it might be necessary for temporary assistance in regaining health and at other times viewed as an undesirable prolongation of life—or a simple supportive care measure that should be a mandatory procedure?

Does the removal of a nasogastric feeding tube from an eighty-year-old permanently comatose patient who has no living will, but the consensus of the family, constitute murder in your view?

If your living will states explicitly that you do not want artificial tube feeding when you are incurable and irreversibly ill, and your doctors decide to not comply with your wishes based on their own value of preserving life regardless of quality, should the doctors be held liable in a court of law for not following your wishes? Always discuss your living will with your doctor. If he or she does not agree with your wishes, find a doctor who does.

A fifty-two-year-old woman has ALS (Lou Gehrig's disease). She has not been able to move her body, arms, or legs for two years and repeatedly begs her husband and daughter to help her end her life. She needs assistance because she is unable to do it herself. Her husband is on the verge of collapse because he dearly loves his wife and knows she is miserable. However, killing is against everything he believes, besides being against the law. What are your feelings about this?

A terminally ill loved one declares repeatedly that he wants to commit suicide but needs your assistance. He seems rational and is not suffering from any treatable depression or discomfort, but he hates every moment of his existence and wants to move on. He is under hospice care so you know an autopsy would not be mandated. He needs to know what pills and how many will do the job. He wants you to get this information and supply him with the pills. What would you do?

Do you think a doctor should comply with the request of a severely depressed AIDS patient who is refusing further antibiotic treatment for his second bout with pneumonia? Discuss.

If a young woman has been rendered permanently comatose and has no advance directives, should the family be able to determine whether to use artificial measures? Discuss.

Do you think that any competent person can refuse treatment even if that refusal could lead to death?

Do you think that there is an ethical difference between starting a life support measure and stopping it after it has been started?

Your loved one is terminally ill with advanced Alzheimer's and needs a hip replacement operation in order to be mobile and more comfortable. You never discussed this possibility with him or her. Would you ask that it be done or avoid the operation and let nature take its course?

Your loved one has advanced Alzheimer's and needs penicillin to alleviate pneumonia. Would you ask that it be done or avoid the treatment and let nature take its course, provided he or she can be kept comfortable?

Your loved one has advanced Alzheimer's, is terminally ill, and requires artificial food and hydration. Would you ask that those measures be implemented or refuse and let nature take its course?

On any given day in your newspaper there are examples of complicated ethical dilemmas. It is important to get in the habit of discussing these situations and letting your views be known to those who may make decisions for you. Some examples follow.

They give high doses of pain-killers to dying, doctors say.

Most Minnesota doctors say they would give high doses of narcotics to dying patients "if necessary to relieve pain," according to a survey released Wednesday by the Minnesota Medical Association. Of the doctors who said they treat terminally ill patients, 85 percent said they would give a higher-than-standard dose to a hypothetical dying cancer patient who was in pain and asked the doctor to "let her die in peace."

The results of the survey, conducted by the association for the Minnesota Board of Medical Examiners, were released in the latest exchange over allegations that the deaths of two terminally ill Twin Cities–area patients last year were "mercy killings." . . . [The report] said there is a consensus among doctors that they should provide adequate pain relief to dying patients, and that doctors already are bound by ethical standards and licensing laws not to commit euthanasia.

The two cases involve the administration of large doses of morphine more than a year ago to a 67-year-old woman at Fairview Southdale Hospital and a 27-year-old St. Paul man at University of Minnesota Hospital, both of whom were very near death. The medical examiner found that the morphine was responsible for the deaths, but the doctors' lawyers quoted experts who said the underlying diseases caused the deaths.

—G. Slovut, *Minneapolis–St. Paul Star Tribune*, 26 April 1990
Reprinted with permission

What do you think about this?

Panel says doctors ethically can help the terminally ill to commit suicide.

Physicians ethically can help terminally ill patients commit suicide by prescribing drugs such as sleeping pills and telling the patients the dosage they would need to end their lives, a blue-ribbon panel of doctors has concluded.

Patient-requested, physician-assisted suicides are "certainly not rare" today, although no one knows the number, says the report in today's *New England Journal of Medicine.*

. . . The group's most important finding is that "we feel most doctors are not adequately and humanely caring for the dying—they are not treating pain and suffering adequately."

The Hennepin County Medical Center doctor said that if more physicians offered such care, there would be many fewer patients wanting to end their lives before the normal disease process brings death.

The doctor emphasized that the panel's statement deals only with cases in which the patient has a relatively short time to live.

—L. Cope, *Minneapolis–St. Paul Star Tribune,* 30 March 1989
Reprinted with permission

What do you think about this?

The Right to Die

The world of religion and philosophy was shocked when Henry P. Van Dusen and his wife ended their lives by their own hands. Dr. Van Dusen had been president of Union Theological Seminary; for more than a quarter-century he had been one of the luminous names in Protestant theology. He enjoyed world status as a spiritual leader. News of the self-inflicted death of the Van Dusens, therefore, was profoundly disturbing to all those who attach a moral stigma to suicide and regard it as a violation of God's laws.

Dr. Van Dusen had anticipated this reaction. He and his wife left behind a letter that may have historic significance. It was very brief, but the essential point it made is now being widely discussed by theologians and could represent the beginning of a reconsideration of traditional religious attitudes toward self-inflicted death. The letter raised a moral issue: does an individual have the obligation to go on living even when the beauty and meaning and power of life are gone?

Henry and Elizabeth Van Dusen had lived full lives. In recent years, they had become increasingly ill, requiring almost continual medical care. Their infirmities were worsening, and they realized they would soon become completely dependent for even the most elementary needs and functions. Under these circumstances little dignity would have been left in life. They didn't like the idea of taking up space in a world with too many mouths and too little food. They believed it was a misuse of medical science to keep them technically alive.

They therefore believed they had the right to decide when to die. In making that decision, they weren't turning against life as the highest value; what they were turning against was the notion that there were no circumstances under which life should be discontinued. . . .

The general reaction to suicide may change as people come to understand that it may be a denial, not an assertion, of moral or religious ethics to allow life to be extended without regard to decency or pride. What moral or religious purpose is celebrated by the annihilation of the human spirit in the triumphant act of keeping the body alive? Why are so many people more readily appalled by an unnatural form of dying than by an unnatural form of living?

"Nowadays," the Van Dusens wrote in their last letter, "it is difficult to die. We feel that this way we are taking will become more usual and acceptable as the years pass. . . .

Of course, the thought of our children and our grandchildren makes us sad, but we still feel that this is the best way and the right way to go. We are both increasingly weak and unwell. . . . We are not afraid to die."

Henry Van Dusen was admired and respected in life. He can be admired and respected in death. "Suicide," said Goethe, "is an incident in human life which, however much disputed and discussed, demands the sympathy of every man, and in every age must be dealt with anew. . . . Death is not the greatest loss in life. The greatest loss is what dies inside us while we live. The unbearable tragedy is to live without dignity or sensitivity."

—Norman Cousins, *Saturday Review*, 14 June 1975
Reprinted with permission of the Norman Cousins Estate

What do you think about this?

Man would refuse ruling to take wife off respirator.

A Minneapolis man said Wednesday that he would refuse to obey if a judge appoints him as his wife's conservator and then orders him to remove her from a life-sustaining respirator.

"I don't think I'd go with that, as a matter of conscience," Oliver Wanglie testified at a hearing in Hennepin County District Court. The hearing is to determine whether he or an independent conservator should be appointed to decide whether to remove Helga Wanglie's respirator. She has been in a persistent vegetative state for more than a year. Both Wanglies are 87.

Officials at Hennepin County Medical Center, where Helga Wanglie is hospitalized, want to remove the respirator, saying there is no hope of recovery. Oliver Wanglie opposes the move. "We're living in hope and faith that a miracle will happen so she can recover," he said.

"I will follow her best interests, [but] I do not want to remove ventilation and snuff out her life," Wanglie replied. He said his decision is based on religious beliefs held by the Wanglies and on her instructions to him earlier that all means should be used to keep her alive.

"Helga Wanglie has been attached to a mechanical breathing device for 17 months, longer than any other comatose patient her doctors know about," said Dr. Steven Miles, a medical ethicist and gerontologist at the hospital who also has treated her.

Her family and doctors agree that she has been in a vegetative state since last May, when she suffered a heart attack and blood flow to her brain stopped for an unknown amount of time. She had been on a respirator before that at Hennepin County because of pneumonia that developed after she fell and broke her hip. Her care, which hospital officials say has cost $800,000, is covered by private insurance. Other insureds are paying for her care in having to pay higher premiums.

The two medical doctors testified yesterday that keeping Wanglie on a respirator is "inappropriate medicine" because her condition is irreversible and the machine will do nothing to cure her or improve her quality of life. Without it, Miles said, she likely will die. He said the irreversible brain damage has destroyed her ability to feel pain or to be aware of her surroundings.

—Warren Wolfe, *Minneapolis–St. Paul Star Tribune*, 29 May 1991
Reprinted with permission

What do you think about this?

How Do Families Start Talking About Their Values?

Self-initiated

Be direct. "I worry about suddenly dying or getting very sick, burdening you with all sorts of confusion and decisions. It would feel better sharing with you what I value and clarify everything I can now." Something like this needs to be said in a straightforward, matter-of-fact way.

Ask for time. Tell the persons you wish to inform what you want to discuss and why. Ask them for a block of their time and set a date so they know you are serious.

Make a list or check those points in this book that you want to go over.

This process can be an opportunity for important modeling. You can make death a comfortable subject in your home. I can distinctly remember when my dad astonished me by saying, "I made a will today and I'm going to talk to you all about it after dinner." I was about fourteen and the mere thought of my dad dying was incomprehensible. I sat silently and aghast at the beginning of the discussion, but gradually lightened up because he was not at all morbid. Quite the contrary, he was obviously delighted with his decisions. It dawned on me, for perhaps the first time, that death is a reality for us all and need not be a taboo subject. It was one of my first lessons on how large a forbidden subject looms until it is aired and opened up for discussion.

Other-initiated

If you are an adult child, a spouse, or a concerned other and want to initiate discussion about health-care issues, several approaches can be taken.

Directly express your concern. Examples: "I get worried sometimes that I wouldn't know how you would feel or what you would want done if certain things happened. I'd want to do what you would wish, but I need to know what those wishes are." "I'm worried that unless you talk to me about some of these matters, I'm going to be left with a terrible mess and decisions to make that wouldn't have to exist if you'd help me think this through now."

Discuss what if's. "What if, down the road, you can't manage in this house any more? What would you like done? What services might help? Have you considered any particular housing option?"

Indirect Approach

Some people flatly refuse any direct approach. Whenever you hear a story about someone else that involves a decision, ask your loved one what he or she thinks about it. For example: Sheila's daughter got an excellent job opportunity out of town. Sheila's sick about it and asked her not to go. What do you think about it? George and Elizabeth have moved into that new high-rise for seniors downtown. What have you heard about it?

This chapter used several approaches to help you clarify for yourself what is important to you. Some of it may have been hard for you to think about because most of us hope we won't ever be in these situations. Congratulate yourself for taking the time because reflection and values clarification provide the foundation for planning responsibly for your future.

4 · Health-Care Planning

After thinking, in chapter 3, about what you value, the next step on your pilgrimage of self-discovery is to gather information and reflect on particular issues regarding your own health care. This chapter begins with inquiries into your personal feelings and experiences with your health. Then it provides information and encourages discussion about controversial late-life issues such as your definition of meaningful life and your feelings about resuscitation, artificial food and hydration, withdrawing versus withholding life supports, euthanasia, and assisted suicide.

It is important to ponder these issues and share your conclusions with someone. Your beliefs may be absolute and certain or may reflect your confusion and uncertainty. But the discussion is necessary for your surrogate decision-maker to make responsible decisions congruent with your wishes, if called for in the future.

Personal Feelings

Your current state of health is . . .

What bothers you most about your health?

Do you have any specific chronic illness(es)?

Are you satisfied with your medical care? If not, how would you like to change it?

Are you usually honest with yourself about your health?

Are you honest with others?

Do you think you pay enough attention to your health?

If you are healthy now, can you project what kind of a patient you'll be when you get sick (stoic, wimpy, resilient)?

How have you wanted to be treated in the past when you were ill?

What are your good health habits?

Do you have bad health habits?

Have you broken any bad health habits? Elaborate.

What can you do about the bad habits you still have? Formulate a health plan for yourself.

What Makes Life Meaningful for You?

Before proceeding, you might wish to review appendixes C and D, which contain a glossary of legal and ethical terms and a glossary of health-care terms, respectively, that might be helpful for you to examine now and to refer to when necessary.

Now that you have explored your feelings about your own health and have looked over the definition of terms in the appendixes, it is time to look in more depth at some of the puzzling and often complicated issues of late life. Be gentle with yourself; these are important but delicate subjects. Technology has forced reconsideration of the definition of death. In the past, when your heart stopped beating and you stopped breathing, you were pronounced dead. Now patients on heart-lung machines are unable to breathe or pump blood on their own but are very much alive. Life-sustaining devices are capable of maintaining heartbeat and respiration in patients who have suffered irreversible loss of brain function. Neurological criteria have been added to the definition of death because of this life-sustaining technology.

The President's Commission for the Study of Ethical Problems in Medicine and Biomedical and Behavioral Research (1983) developed the Uniform Determination of Death Act (UDDA), which specified two alternate criteria for determining death. The UDDA reads as follows: An individual who has sustained either an (1) irreversible cessation of circulatory and respiratory functions, or (2) irreversible cessation of all functions of the entire brain, including the brain stem, is dead. A determination of death must be made in accordance with accepted medical standards. The UDDA recognizes that death can still be determined by the traditional breathing/heartbeat criteria in the majority of cases, but also covers artificially maintained cardiopulmonary function with the inclusion of neurological criteria. Even this definition of death leaves many questions and is still very controversial. There is an ongoing debate between the "whole-brain"

(UDDA definition) and "higher brain" theorists, who believe that the criterion for death is the irreversible loss of the capacity for consciousness and social interaction. According to those who believe in the higher brain concept of death, persons in a persistent vegetative state (PVS) would be considered dead even though the brain stem is still functioning. A person in this state requires artificial food and hydration, often does not require a respirator, and can live for a long time (thirty-seven years is the record).

It is important to think about these types of issues in a time when machines can keep you organically alive beyond the body's natural abilities. How you personally define death and how you define quality of life are the two questions at the crux of many decisions you may be asked to make.

Ask yourself what specific mental and social functions you feel are essential to being human. At what point does human life end and only physiologic activity remain? Does being human include the capacity to remember, to reason, to have sensory awareness, to be conscious? Does life have to do with maintaining your identity, your sense of psychological continuity and connectedness?

What is meaningful life—life that should be continued? Under what circumstances would life no longer be meaningful to you?

The objective of this chapter is to start you thinking and talking about a very complex matter. You may have settled on a comfortable description of what meaningful life is, or you may be more confused but wiser, recognizing that defining death is complicated and that your belief system plays an integral part in assessing what it means to you. Would your grandparents ever have believed that there would be a day when there would be no consensus about what it means to be dead?

Resuscitation

Cardiopulmonary resuscitation (CPR) is an emergency intervention designed to restore heartbeat and breathing. Procedures range from mouth-to-mouth resuscitation to sophisticated electrical defibrillation (electric shock to the heart), use of drugs, and open-chest cardiac massage. It is now being recognized that although CPR is wonderfully successful sometimes, there are often poor outcomes and CPR should not be universally administered. Medical and gerontological journals repeatedly report grim statistics on the use of CPR with frail elderly persons. Even when life is technically saved, patients are often reduced to a questionable quality of life, confined to intensive care units or nursing homes, requiring constant care.

Do not resuscitate (DNR) is a medical order made by a physician to withhold CPR in the case of cardiac arrest, either because the physician deems the patient such a poor risk that there would be no medical benefit and that any medical treatment would be futile, or because the patient or surrogate decision-maker for the patient believes that, even if revived, the quality of life would be unacceptable.

CPR is routinely administered in most situations when someone experiences cardiac or respiratory arrest. There is a presumption favoring the preservation of life, regardless of a person's general physical condition, and a corresponding legal presumption that assumes patient consent to CPR. It is important to realize that CPR occurs automatically in emergency situations unless there is a DNR order in place. This policy of automatically administering CPR appears to be changing as more data verify the medical complications of resuscitation, including trauma to the chest as well as severe and chronic, irreversible neurological damage. Persons receiving CPR fall into three categories:

1. CPR should be given to patients who overdose, who have ventricular arrhythmias, heart attacks, anesthesia complications, or to any basically healthy person who suffers an unexpected trauma. There is a 20 to 50 percent chance of recovery with this group.

2. Poor results are generally seen in persons over seventy who receive CPR and who suffer from advanced chronic disease such as cerebral vascular disease, cirrhosis, chronic lung disease, and so on. This group shows a poor statistical probability of ultimate survival (less than 10 percent). Persons in this category should discuss DNR orders with those close to them and with their doctor. The physician needs to outline explicitly the pros and cons of treatment options, so that the best possible decision can be made about the patient's future.

3. For persons with irreversible illness, patients who suffer with multiple organ failure or unresponsive metastatic cancer, many professionals counsel that CPR should not be given or even considered, the family should be advised of the futility of this approach, and a DNR order should be written.

DNR orders should be carefully discussed. What does "quality of life" mean to a particular person? If he or she is in a high-risk category, the physician should discuss with the family the odds of recovery and projections of quality of life if CPR is given. Only by questioning your physician will you get enough information to make a well-informed decision. If DNR is decided upon, orders should be placed in the person's medical record and hospital chart. The DNR order should be part of the care plan with specific, written instructions on what should and should not be done and these decisions should be discussed with key caregivers. Nurses should not only know what to do but also the rationale for the decision so that they can answer questions and ease worries that the patient or family may have. DNR orders should be reviewed on a regular basis in case there is any pertinent change in health status or the patient or family has any qualms that need to be addressed.

A major concern is that a DNR order means that the patient will be abandoned, ignored, or receive less care. Special attention needs to be given to alleviate this fear. Patients with DNR orders need to understand that they will receive comfort care and that every effort will be made to minimize suffering. A DNR order does not mean that other therapies will be withheld. We all need to remember that fear of abandonment and fear of dying don't just go away. An individual's fears need to be verbalized, questions need to be asked, and therapeutic options need to be thoroughly discussed. It is critical to alleviate these fears and to understand that, if you are the patient, you will be kept comfortable.

Artificial Food and Hydration

Laws regarding artificial feeding vary from state to state. It is best if you state definitively in your advance directive how you feel about this matter.

It is important to distinguish between artificial food and hydration and eating and drinking. The food and liquid that you put in your mouth are eating and drinking. Prepared products artificially put into your system are considered medical treatment and can extend your life, depending on the circumstance, for many years. These products can be administered in the form of intravenous sugar and water (hydration), hyperalimentation (under local anesthesia a needle is placed in the subclavian vein and prepared fluids are administered), or through a tube, either nasogastrically (tube through nose to stomach) or gastrostomically (tube surgically implanted directly into stomach).

Artificial nutrition and hydration can only be given with a doctor's order and the consent of the patient or the patient's surrogate. It is an extremely beneficial treatment in the recovery of some persons. It is also considered by many an unnecessary treatment for persons with no hope of recovery, only extending the dying process. Keep in mind that life-support discussions occur when further treatment is considered futile and the patient is unable to make his or her own decisions. According to Joanne Lynn and James Childress, at this point, patients who are allowed to die without artificial hydration and nutrition may sometimes die more comfortably than those who receive it.

Sometimes when a serious or life-threatening accident involves a formerly active, healthy person, artificial food and hydration are given on a time-limited basis to enable adequate assessment of the medical condition or to help the family adjust to the suddenness of the need for decision-making and to decide whether the situation is indeed futile. In 1986, the American Medical Association issued a major opinion: "It is not unethical to discontinue all means of life-prolonging medical treatment. Life-prolonging medical treatment includes medication and artificially or technologically supplied respiration, nutrition and hydration."

The question of the morality of discontinuing artificial food and hydration continues. Estimates range from twenty-five thousand to sixty thousand Americans who exist in a persistent vegetative state (PVS) and are maintained by tubal feedings. It cost $131,000 per year to keep Karen Ann Quinlan in this state. Another woman was kept in a vegetative state for thirty-seven years at the cost of $16,000 per month, according to some estimates. Despite one court ruling after another stating that artificial feeding and hydration are medical procedures similar to artificial breathing by means of a respirator, feelings about this particular set of life-prolonging measures are varied and intense. It is important to determine how you feel about this issue, to be sure that your surrogate decision-maker knows what your feelings are, and to choose a doctor who will follow your wishes.

Eating and drinking symbolize love and caring to many people and most cannot make the distinction between eating and drinking and artificial nutrition and hydration. If this is a person's belief, it is important that it be stated. Many people also recall their own experiences of hunger or thirst and imagine that dying from malnutrition and dehydration must be pure agony, no matter what they are told to the contrary. Kidney dialysis machines and respirators are equally foreign technology, but they simply do not engender the same value-laden, emotional response as giving or withholding artificial food and hydration.

Receiving artificial food and hydration can be beneficial in some instances and in other circumstances can actually cause pain and suffering, as reported by J. V. Zerwekh, the President's Commission, and J. Lynn and J. F. Childress.

Excess fluid puts strain on the heart and kidneys already weakened by the illness and sometimes causes vomiting and difficulties with breathing.

Nutrients also can create complications when someone is extremely ill.

The gastrostomy is an operation requiring general anesthesia, usually relatively simple with little aftercare required, but sometimes the incision can become infected and cause discomfort.

Claustrophobic panic and confusion sometimes occur when one has tubes in the nose and throat. In addition, when patients try to remove the tubes, they are often placed in restraints, which magnifies the feelings of helplessness and panic.

The tubes in the nose and throat are sometimes annoying, causing additional pain and some risk of pneumonia.

Frail elderly persons often have very thin veins, making it difficult and painful to insert needles for intravenous feedings.

The cost of prolonging death by these procedures can cause emotional and financial suffering to the family.

Patients maintained in this manner can be kept alive for years. They typically develop contracture of the knees, elbows, and hips and stiffen in a fetal position. Bed sores are hard to prevent.

Is it painful to die if artificial food and hydration are withheld or withdrawn? No. Observation and medical evidence indicates that there is no pain when patients are this near to death. Various reports concur that death occurs peacefully within three to fourteen days (J. V. Zerwekh, the President's Commission, J. Lynn and J. F. Childress, AMA Opinion). Since the beginning of time, people have been dying of malnutrition and dehydration as a result of famine, disease, or deliberate decision. In the last few days of the lives of most people who have been sick for a period of time, they typically choose not to eat much. This used to be considered a "natural death," but in recent years intravenous feedings and nasogastric tube feeding and gastrostomies have become a much used option. Now patients can be maintained for decades on artificial feeding, kidney dialysis, and mechanical ventilators. Some think this sounds like a fate worse than death; others choose to live as long as possible, regardless of the quality of life. What are your views regarding artificial food and hydration?

Withdrawing Versus Withholding

Another psychological stumbling block for many is whether there is a difference between discontinuing artificial food and hydration and not starting it in the first place. There is no difference, ethically or legally; both have the same result. It would be more helpful to put aside these terms and focus on "termination of treatment." Families sometimes need time to adjust, and it is comforting to know that tube feeding can be used temporarily to help with this process. Then, when it is apparent the treatment is futile and the dying process is simply being prolonged, tube feeding can be stopped.

For those who think that there is a distinction between withholding and withdrawing artificial food and hydration, two scenarios tend to predominate. Either patients are kept on artificial feeding and nutrition for as long as it takes for death to occur or the treatment is refused initially because of the fear that the treatment will not be able to be stopped once it starts. It is wise to ask how your physician views this matter. If you do not have similar beliefs, you should find a doctor who concurs. It is advisable to address this issue in your advance directive and discuss it with your surrogate: "I consider artificial food and hydration an ordinary comfort measure and I do not want it withdrawn or withheld" or "I consider artificial food and hydration to be medical procedures similar to the use of a respirator and when further treatment is considered futile and it would not add to my discomfort, I would want this form of treatment withheld or withdrawn."

Life Extension

So now you can be kept alive! Is this what you want? Under what circumstances? Advanced industrial democracies are in a stage of societal development in which their members no longer die of acute illnesses but of delayed degenerative diseases characterized by late onset and slow decline. According to M. P. Battin, this situation applies to 70 to 80 percent of the population and presents altogether new dilemmas and a shift of emphasis on quality of life questions.

It is important to note with all this talk about choices at the frail end of life, most health-care decisions throughout life are clear-cut. Most medical care does not require any ethical decision-making because the decisions do not need to be debated when using sound medical knowledge. For instance, respirators are routinely used as temporary, normal recovery devices after some operations. This choice is not debatable because there is consensus that it is sound medical practice and a transient part of treatment. Patients usually recover and return to normal lives.

New technological advances and the complexities of dealing with multiple variables of degenerative disease place doctors and patients in morally ambiguous situations concerning the dying process. New and tough decisions are needed when the risks or costs aren't clear, the patient's desires may differ from the physician's or family's, or it is not clear who should decide.

Medical decisions are prospective, and in that regard, they differ from decisions made in law, which are based on previous cases. Medical decisions are based on what will happen and involve weighing the risks and the benefits and then trusting the process. Every situation is different and can change as new variables are introduced. For example, kidney dialysis is a process used to remove unwanted fluid and waste products from the body when the kidneys are unable to do so naturally. The blood is purified by being pumped from a patient's artery through a kidney machine and returned to the body through the patient's vein. When people have a serious kidney disease or when the kidneys fail, a typical response is to provide the patient with dialysis as a means of compensating for loss of kidney function. This is a highly appreciated and effective wonder of modern science and people can enjoy a decent quality of life with this treatment. The use of dialysis comes becomes problematic, however, when a person has other complications such as a stroke or heart failure which place a severe strain on the kidneys. Only then does the question of whether the use of dialysis is simply prolonging the person's dying arise. Then the burdens may outweigh the benefits and the dialysis may make no positive contribution.

When trying to decide on the value of a treatment, ask yourself: What if this were me? If a therapy would help you recover or maintain an acceptable state, it would probably be worth it. If the treatment would hurt you and only prolong your dying, you would have to make a judgment based on your value system.

With technology and social values constantly changing, medicine and morality cannot be fixed in stone .

Ordinary and extraordinary means are not legitimate terms any longer because what was extraordinary yesterday has become ordinary today. The terms put the focus solely on the means (e.g., IV feeding tubes, respirators) instead of on the impact of the means on the total person. The question to ask is, "Will the negatives, the burdens, outweigh the benefits of the treatment?" Opponents of withholding and withdrawing treatment (sometimes called passive euthanasia) and certainly opponents of active euthanasia often lean on the fact that these approaches to death violate the Hippocratic Oath. Margaret P. Battin points out that the original Greek version of the oath also prohibits performing surgery and taking fees for teaching medicine, neither of which survived into contemporary medical practice.

Euthanasia

Euthanasia is the active killing of a person for reasons thought to be merciful. Euthanasia and assisted suicide are two potential approaches to the dying process that are illegal, very controversial, and are sure to be the subject of much medical and ethical discourse in the future. Much more open discussion and information are needed before any kind of decisions can be made regarding the legalization of these approaches.

Different cultures have different outlooks on these issues. Battin has reported that Dutch physicians see performing euthanasia on individuals who request it when nothing else can be done to relieve the patient's condition as a part of their duty not a violation of it. She goes on to say that in the Netherlands, where active voluntary euthanasia is accepted, the guidelines state that:

1. the patient's request be voluntary and an enduring, reflective one versus a transitory impulse;

2. the patient be undergoing intolerable suffering;

3. all alternatives acceptable to the patient for relieving the suffering have been tried;

4. the patient has full information and understands it;

5. the physician has consulted with a second physician whose judgment can be expected to be independent.

Advocates of euthanasia say it is more humane to end a painful life in a dying patient than to watch, over time, a protracted illness; persons have a right to choose their own death at their own time; and there is no moral difference between allowing a patient to die, as, for example, by withholding or withdrawing nutrition and hydration, and actively killing a patient, if death is the expected outcome. F. J. Brescia outlines the opposing views, drawn from the following concepts: life is a gift from God and it is always wrong to kill because of the sanctity of life; the role of medicine is to seek life, not death; and the consequences of legalizing medical practices toward mercy killing move us away from the moral absolute against killing and logically down the path of social abuse. It is believed by those who espouse the last argument that any support for euthanasia starts society down the slippery slope from practicing it on those who meet the criteria now to those who don't, such as elderly persons and persons with disabilities.

Ideas about the dying process and who should make the decisions have definitely evolved. Whether this has resulted from a gradual adjustment to new situations or is, indeed, a demonstration of the "slippery slope" in action is a matter of opinion. At one time not so long ago, doctors made most decisions for their patients. Now there is more emphasis on self-direction and autonomy. This shift brings with it enormous responsibility and an increasing respect for the complexity and vast gray area of these decisions. One story moves you in one direction; another, the opposite. The important thing is to open yourself to discussion and to struggling with these issues. What are the values upon which you lean when making such decisions? What are your views on euthanasia?

Physician-Assisted Suicide

Physician-assisted suicide is an act in which a doctor gives a patient the means and specific instructions by which to take his or her own life. There remain instances in which incurably ill patients suffer intolerably before death despite comprehensive efforts to provide pain relief and comfort. Consider the following patients: a man with ALS (Lou Gehrig's disease) who has been quadriplegic for years and no longer wants to linger captive in his body, dependent and praying for death; a woman with oral cancer who has a gaping, foul-smelling wound, who can no longer eat, and no longer wants to fight; and a man with progressive pulmonary fibrosis, who doesn't want to be maintained on a ventilator but is equally terrified of suffocating. These people would rather die than live and feel that there should be "aid in dying." Perhaps groups like the American Medical Association and the National Hospice Organization can help by creating guidelines for terminal sedation in special cases of uncontrollable symptoms. Many feel that there should be a law recognizing the individual's right, under certain circumstances, to seek and obtain assistance in ending life.

The basic argument in favor of assisted suicide's legality runs as follows: Competent individuals have the right to refuse treatment, including life-sustaining treatment, with full knowledge and acceptance that death will ensue. In respecting these wishes, physicians may commit an intentional act—such as removal of a respirator—that results in a patient's death, thereby assisting the patient to do what is necessary for death to occur. Patients may receive medication intended to relieve pain even though its unavoidable, known, and accepted consequence is the unintended hastening of death.

Given this state of the law, the argument goes, there is no logical reason why a competent, terminally ill patient, fully informed of the facts and consequences of such a decision, may not ask a physician to commit the purposeful act of providing medication intended to end the patient's life, when that patient decides that life has become an unendurable existence. G. Scofield argues that, beyond satisfying the patient's right of self-determination, this act promotes beneficence because it ends a patient's pain and suffering. Assisted suicide is the next step in the legal evolution of autonomy and respecting an individual's choice, according to this line of thinking.

Scofield also explains the opposition, who say that "the nature of the act, intent, and chain of causation involved in assisted suicide differs significantly. . . . Death is not accidental, natural, or even the result of unintended iatrogenic complications; it is chemically induced. . . . Writing out a prescription with the intent that it be used to end life is not like entering a DNR order. Even the nature of the patient's request is different. One asks for interventions to cease; the other that medicine directly intervene to make death occur. One risks, the other seeks, death."

This is a complicated issue; there are ardent supporters and opponents in the debate over legalizing physician-assisted suicide. Dr. Jack Kevorkian's notoriety as he repeatedly assisted people who chose to kill themselves, and the best selling, how-to-commit-suicide book *Final Exit* promise to keep this controversial issue in the forefront. What are your thoughts about physician-assisted suicide?

Costs of and Accessibility to Health Care

Major issues on the political agenda are the cost and accessibility of health care. Thirty-one million Americans in 1992 had no health insurance. The consensus seems to be that health care changes need to be made, but resounding controversy continues around just what these changes should be. As the ability to perform "medical miracles" increases, individuals are forced not only to make personal decisions, but societal ones as well. Technological advances carry a high price tag. For example, women with breast cancer have years added to their lives by having bone marrow transplants at the cost of $100,000 per year. It costs $850 per day or $310,000 per year to keep a person on a respirator. In 1993 in an article entitled "Who Can Afford a Nursing Home?" *Consumer Reports* listed the cost of a year in a nursing home as between $22,000 and $35,000 and projected costs to double in the next thirty years. Should there be limited access to expensive procedures and life-saving devices?

Federal and state governments grapple with a myriad of complex questions regarding universal access, methods of funding, equitable distribution of costs, and prioritization of medical procedures to be covered. The questions are unending. It is important to stay abreast of the controversies and let your opinions be known to your appropriate political representatives.

Conclusion

When do you think enough is enough as far as life support measures are concerned? How you feel about artificial food and hydration, withdrawing versus withholding treatment, assisted suicide, euthanasia, and the costs and accessibility of health care? Once you consider these issues, you are ready to prepare an advance directive.

5 · Advance Directives

During the 1970s and 1980s, an outcry arose from people fearful that their lives might be extended far beyond quality years or their ability to think. They feared for themselves and they feared for their families. They demanded a mechanism to save them legally from what they considered unwanted life extension. By 1993, all states and the District of Columbia had responded to this demand by legalizing one or both forms of advance directives: the living will or durable power of attorney for health care. These are legal documents that allow competent individuals to retain some control over health-care decisions in the event they are no longer able to do so in the future.

In 1990, Congress enacted the Patient Self-Determination Act (PSDA), which requires hospitals, health maintenance organizations, home health-care providers, and nursing facilities to advise patients of their rights to make health-care decisions in advance by using advance directives. The PSDA opens the expectation of choice, but, since it does not require a process of exploration of the patient's values, facilities merely ask, "Do you have an advance directive?" Many talk supportively about these self-management documents, but few act. The living will and durable power of attorney for health care will be discussed in detail in this chapter and you are encouraged to take the time to actually fill in the forms provided in the appendix. These documents are not ends in themselves. Careful thought and reflection are integral to the process of completing the documents.

Why not avoid this gloomy subject?

- "I don't need to think about this. I'm just going to die the 'good old fashioned way'."
- "It won't happen to me."
- "This is morbid. Who wants to think about dying?"
- "Who cares? It'll be someone else's problem."
- "I'll do it next year. I'm feeling fine."
- "I'm afraid to sign one of those things. No one will take care of me then."
- "Other people know better than I do what is best."
- "I trust my doctor to know."
- "I trust my children/spouse to do the right thing for me if something should happen and I couldn't decide for myself."
- "No one would pay any attention to it anyway."
- "It will only cause conflict in my family. If I pick one child over another to be my proxy, it would make the others feel bad."
- "You can't possibly anticipate how you are going to die. Trying to do so will only confuse things."

Sound familiar?

Your body will not last forever. That is a simple fact. What isn't simple is that dying is more complicated today than it used to be. People used to get sick and die. No problem. No decisions. It is different today because of the wonders of technology, better preventative knowledge, and life-style choices. Your expectations of later life have changed. Now people get sick and can reasonably expect to be made well or better. For the most part, the changes have been wonderful. Older people are healthier longer. Generally, a person who is eighty today is comparable physically to a person who was sixty-five years of age thirty years ago. Years have literally been added to our lives and life added to our years.

With these added years of living, families find themselves dealing with dynamics that did not formerly exist. Adult children are finding that they have to work on parental relationships and be honest about their feelings because they are no longer "saved" by their aging parents' early departure from their lives. The added time either gives older people a great deal more to avoid and deny or the opportunity to make some changes for the better, to live life more fully, complete with all its pain, suffering, joy, wonder, and tenderness.

Why do you have to think about this?

1. According to an article entitled "Focus: Living Wills" in *Good Age* magazine, the majority of Americans will be faced with these kinds of decisions. In 1991, approximately 2.1 million Americans died and 1.7 million of them died in a

health-care facility. Of those 1.7 million deaths, 70 percent involved decisions about whether to withdraw or withhold life-support systems.

> *The time of death—once a matter of fate—*
> *is now a matter of human choice. . . .*
> *Nearly every death involves a decision*
> *whether to take some medical procedure*
> *that could prolong the process of dying.*
> —Supreme Court Justice Brennan in the Nancy Cruzan case

2. There are new questions. Technology can keep parts of you alive. It is now your decision whether and in what circumstances mechanical interventions should be used or withdrawn. Obviously you cannot know precisely what your dying circumstances will be. But you can let your general views be known to your doctor and those to whom it is important and alleviate the pressure they will feel if they don't know. You need information, you need definitions of terms, and you need time to think about and discuss these weighty decisions.

3. Spare your family members the anguish of not knowing how you would feel about these matters. Being open to discussing these issues is a responsible and loving gesture to your survivors. Making them guess what you prefer leads families into difficult, divisive times that can be avoided by some thoughtful self-investigation and preplanning. If you have complete faith in your physician's decision-making and for this reason decline to make out an advance directive, let this decision be known to your family. Doctors do not want to get involved in family dynamics and prefer to speak to one decision-maker. So it is advisable for you to choose a single proxy and an alternate who can best articulate your views. Since this can be a delicate matter, explain to your family the necessity of having one decision-maker and who you have designated as your surrogate so that they will not be surprised later.

4. You don't know specifically how you are going to die, but if your wishes and values on quality of life matters are known, you have a much better chance of being medically treated as you would prefer. According to S. H. Wanser, S. J. Adelstein, and R. E. Cranford, "the principal obstacle to a patient's effective participation in decision-making is lack of competence, and only when competence is lacking can others substitute their judgment for that of the patient. If the terminally ill patient's ability to make decisions becomes progressively reduced, the physician must rely increasingly on the presumed or prestated wishes of the patient. It helps if there is a longstanding relationship between patient and physician, but in fact many adults have no personal physician. Terminally ill patients are often cared for by specialists or members of house staff who do not know what the patient would have wished."

5. Without preplanning, others may make decisions about your welfare inconsistent with what you would wish.

W. H. Colby reported that in *Nancy Cruzan v. State of Missouri*, the U. S. Supreme Court's 1990 decision upheld the Missouri court's decision to refuse to withdraw feeding tubes from Nancy Cruzan, who had been in a vegetative state since a 1983 automobile accident. The decision stated that there was not "clear and convincing evidence" that this would be her wish. Her parents wanted the hospital to remove the feeding tubes and allow Nancy to die, but the hospital refused to do so because she had never written down her wishes nor discussed the possibility with friends or family. In *O'Connor v. State of New York*, the New York Court of Appeals ruled in 1988 that an elderly woman being cared for in the Westchester County Medical Center who had repeatedly told others while still competent that she would not want her life prolonged by artificial means, did not provide "clear and convincing" enough evidence to warrant withholding artificial nutrition and hydration. The court determined that her statements were merely "immediate reactions to the unsettling experience of seeing or hearing of another's unnecessarily prolonged death." These two cases, along with many others, have impressed many Americans with the urgency of making clear health care declarations.

In this litigious society, when a sole surrogate decision maker has not been designated and there is even a suggestion of discomfort and lack of consensus in a family, medical professionals will most likely choose life support measures for a patient. If you sense that your survivors might disagree over decisions concerning your health, it is even more important that you clearly designate who is to be your official spokesperson.

Living Will

A living will is a written statement, signed by you and witnesses, which gives guidance to your family and doctor about your health-care wishes in preparation for a time when you might not be able to make decisions yourself. It is sometimes referred to as an advance directive for health care. You can state whether you do or do not want to undergo particular life-prolonging medical procedures when your condition is considered irreversible and terminal. It is important to note that in many states, a living will only goes into effect when you are in a terminal condition. The durable power of attorney for health care, discussed in the next section, is activated if you are in a nonterminal or terminal condition but unable to make or communicate your health-care wishes.

Many states have legislated guidelines for advance directives, and while specific provisions vary from state to state, they all generally authorize a "competent adult" to execute a declaration in advance, stating his or her intent about health-care preferences. A proxy decision-maker can also be named in many states' living will forms. This designated proxy will make medical decisions on your behalf if you become unable to make them yourself. A living will document provides a vehicle to ensure that those decisions are made in accordance with your preferences and, since they are written for all to see, the surrogate decision-maker need feel no remorse over carrying out your wishes.

Can I change my living will once it has been signed and witnessed? Yes. A living will can be revoked at any time and it is advisable to renew it on a regular basis. Situations change; your living situation, health, or even a relationship may change, warranting an update of your living will.

How is it determined whether one is competent to make his or her own decisions? Usually your attending doctor, a psychologist, or a neurologist determines your capacity to make health-care decisions. Legally, a patient is considered competent to make a treatment decision if he or she has the ability to understand relevant information about the medical problem and the consequences of the decisions about treatment. With dementia, there is a progressive loss of decision-making ability that makes assessment complicated. Assessment often involves "ruling out" any possibility of other causal factors, such as tumors, infection, or possible drug reactions, creating the cognitive impairment. There is no consensus concerning a particular standard for assessment of decision-making ability, but P. S. Appelbaum and L. H. Roth outline several agreed-upon factors that should be taken into consideration during evaluation:

- Evaluation should include reports from reliable informants other than the patient and from direct observation and testing of the patient.
- Evaluation should ideally take place in the patient's home and be made over several visits to take into account fluctuating decision-making ability and coherence of content over time.
- Whereas there is no single psychometric test available to assess decision-making ability, there are tests that can be used as part of the evaluation.

To determine whether a person is able to make decisions, it is important for families to ask whether the person is making decisions consistent with underlying values previously expressed and whether the choices being made promote the individual's well-being as he or she sees it.

Is a special living will form required in your state? Yes. Every state and the District of Columbia has some form of advance directive. They do vary from state to state and have different requirements. You can write or call Choice in Dying, Inc., for a state-specific form and information:

> Choice in Dying, Inc.
> 200 Varick Street
> New York, New York 10014-4810
> 212-366-5540 or 1-800-989-WILL (9455)

You can also receive specific information on your state's requirements by calling the agency for your state (listed in appendix F) and asking to speak to your state legal service developer. Ask for a form, instructions for its use, and whether there are sample forms provided to assist you.

What if I spend half of my time in one state and half in another? To be safe, write two living wills. Get forms for both states.

What do I do with the living will after it is executed? Give copies to your doctor, proxy, family, clergy, lawyer, and anyone else closely associated with you. Put the original in an accessible place—not your safe deposit box. Check to see that it is in the official care plan if you are in a hospital or nursing home.

Should you discuss your living will with anyone? You are not legally required to do so, but it is strongly encouraged. A living will serves as an excellent discussion catalyst for subjects not considered or reflected upon in many households. Such a discussion will also give your family and your physician the chance to ask any questions they might have and let you know whether they are comfortable following your wishes. Remember that the major value of the living will is the discussion itself—letting others know what you think about these critical issues.

What about the "extra protection" of a proxy appointment? If at all possible, you should also name a person you trust and who knows you well to make medical decisions in accordance with your wishes if the time comes when you cannot make them for yourself. The proxy appointment is the most important part of the living will because it allows you to designate someone to implement on-the-spot decisions as you would wish them to be made. It enables you to have someone "stand in your shoes" to discuss treatment alternatives when you cannot speak for yourself.

What types of treatment should you think about? You should consider what types of life-prolonging procedures would or would not be acceptable to you and under what conditions. These procedures include cardiac resuscitation, radiation, dialysis, antibiotics that cannot realistically improve your chances of recovery, respirator treatment, chemotherapy, and artificial feeding and hydration.

How specific should you be? There is great danger in over-medicalizing or over-specification in advance directives. Since you cannot know the details about how you will eventually die, discussing specific interventions without clarity about the context of those actions obscures the issue and lessens the chances of your wishes being respected. It is better that your trusted surrogate and your doctor understand your general views and then be able to apply them to decisions that have to be made. For advance directives to be most effective and workable, focus on the process. Statements such as "Never let me die" or "Never put me on a respirator or feeding tube" can effectively negate your wishes because the statements are too extreme to be considered medically sound and physicians can override them.

What if my doctor doesn't agree with my wishes and choices? Your wishes should prevail unless they are out of the bounds of reasonable medical practice. If, after thoughtful discussion, your doctor does not agree with your preferences for treatment, he or she is obligated to make a reasonable effort to transfer you to a doctor who will respect your rights.

What if my family or friends disagree with my treatment choices? Here, too, your wishes should prevail. But your family will be less likely to disagree if they can discuss your preferences with you and get a clear idea of your reasoning. Pick a spokesperson (proxy) who will carry out your wishes and, if you suspect that there will be objections by someone in particular, acknowledge that in writing.

If you refuse life-sustaining treatment, will you still be taken care of?
Yes. Living will laws usually state that comfort or palliative care should be provided, which includes medication for pain, nursing and hygienic care, and other treatment administered for the purpose of keeping you as comfortable and free from pain as possible.

Appendix E contains two sample living wills: one form that is currently used in eleven states (Delaware, Massachusetts, Michigan, Nebraska, New Jersey, New Mexico, New York, Ohio, Pennsylvania, Rhode Island, and South Dakota) and the other from Minnesota (along with suggestions for filling it out). It also includes a durable power of attorney for health care form. You might use these forms or call your state's designated agency (listed in appendix F) to obtain the updated state-specific living will and/or durable power of attorney for health care documents and determine the current requirements of your state.

Durable Power of Attorney for Health Care

The durable power of attorney for health care (DPAHC) is a legal document written for the purpose of designating another person (the agent) to make health-related decisions on your behalf if, in the judgment of the attending physician, you are unable to do so yourself. This document is comparable to the proxy designation of a living will and is preferable to the living will if your state does not provide the opportunity for proxy designation. Unlike the living will, which in many states applies only when the patient is deemed terminal, the DPAHC enables the designated agent to make decisions if the principal is temporarily or permanently unable to make decisions. Check to see if your state has a statute that authorizes this document. Some states have a durable power of attorney that applies only to property matters; in others, the advance directive for health care document takes precedence.

The person in your state to ask for this information is the state legal service developer (see appendix F). Ask about the details. What are the eligibility requirements for the designated agent? What are the responsibilities of the agent and the designated health-care facility? How is decisional incapacity certified? What legal penalties are associated with failure to obey laws on advance directives? Can it be revoked? What are the specific requirements about witnesses, recording, or notarizing?

Make sure it is clear what you want to accomplish with a DPAHC. This could include accessing medical information and records, employing and discharging medical personnel, refusing or consenting to specific procedures, requesting pain relief, or arranging for care and lodging in a hospital, nursing home, or hospice. Make sure that you clearly inform your agent of your values and wishes. Go over part 2 in this book with your agent. Just as with the living will, think about what you could tell someone that would help him or her make decisions in your best interest, knowing that it is not possible to predict all circumstances that might occur. Remember that in most states it is especially important to specify in writing your feelings about artificial food and hydration.

Whom do you wish to designate as your surrogate? Find out if the person(s) is willing to serve. Not everyone is willing to assume the potential ethical and emotional burdens that can be involved. Keep in mind that the person you designate will have a great deal of power over your health care if you become incapacitated. Also, if you have both a living will and a DPAHC, be sure to designate the same person to be your surrogate decision-maker to avoid confusion.

Once an advance directive is completed, give a copy to your health-care providers and other close family and friends. A copy should be included in your medical records for accessibility and it should be reviewed and updated on a regular basis.

Should I have both a living will and a durable power of attorney for health care? It is important to state your wishes and preferences about health care and it is important to designate an agent or proxy decision-maker. If you can do that in one document in your state, that will be all you need. It is usually advisable to fill out both documents to cover all the contingencies. Remember, in most states the living will only applies if you are in a terminal condition. The DPAHC is activated by decisional incapacity alone—whether you are terminally ill or temporarily or chronically unable to make decisions for yourself—such as being in a persistent vegetative state or an advanced state of dementia.

What if I change my mind? You can revoke the DPAHC by: 1) destroying it (and any copies); 2) creating a written, dated statement to supersede the DPAHC; 3) verbally announcing to two witnesses (who don't need to be present at the same time) that you no longer want the DPAHC to be in effect; and 4) writing a new one.

Who Makes Health-Care Decisions for You?

You do. As long as you have decision-making capacity, you have the autonomy to make your own decisions. All persons who have the ability to understand relevant information about their medical problems and the consequences of the decisions about treatment have the right to decide what can be done to their own bodies. This means that you have the right to refuse treatment of any sort—even the most minor treatment.

Legally, you have the right of "informed consent" to medical treatment, which means that you have the right to be fully informed about a given medical procedure before you agree to it—and before the doctor performs it. Your right to refuse treatment is based on the constitutional right of privacy. Many judges have ruled that your decision to refuse procedures that will only prolong your dying is such a personal one that it can only be restricted when there is a compelling reason, such as responsibility for minor children.

Informed consent is the ideal and stated policy, but in reality often isn't so, sometimes shouldn't be so, and is terribly complicated. As J. Severance reports, it has been estimated that in only 54 percent of cases is the patient actually the primary decision-maker. With the explosion in numbers of persons over the age of eighty-five, there is a corresponding increase in the percentage of persons suffering from Alzheimer's and related diseases, which precludes, along with other illnesses, relying solely on the autonomy model of decision-making. Following are examples that demonstrate how informed consent is not always ideal:

1. A ninety-year-old man who has filled out a living will stating he does not wish any artificial support if incapacitated has a massive stroke but comes to consciousness long enough to be asked if he would like a ventilator. In his foggy state, he feebly answers "yes," negating his advance directive. His children were saddened to see his dying process drag on and felt he had not been truly competent to make a decision congruent with his lifelong values. What do you think?

2. A very ill sixty-five-year-old woman with cancer of the colon initially rejects the possibility of chemotherapy. Her doctor and children urge her to reconsider. She doesn't want to disappoint anyone so she changes her mind. Did she give informed consent? The treatment makes her very ill and she complains that the doctor skewed the information he gave to her and her children about the possible side effects of the chemotherapy. If the doctor, in fact, did not give her enough information or accurate information, did she give informed consent?

There are times when your capacity for judgment may be altered by a variety of circumstances and you may not be competent to make medical decisions. To protect your rights in such a situation, it will be necessary to rely on your prestated wishes, written in the form of an advance directive.

Advance directives. People able to make their own decisions prepare a written directive, stating their wishes in the event that they become unable to make decisions.

Substituted judgment standard An able person has let his or her wishes be known before incapacitation and has designated a surrogate decision-maker to carry out those wishes.

A best-interest standard. This standard is invoked when another person's thoughts are simply not known. Someone is appointed by the physician or family to make decisions based on normative thinking—decisions consistent with what most reasonable individuals, given the same circumstances, would choose. Patients who never had decision-making capacity, such as those with severe mental disabilities and infants, fall into this category.

Conclusion

This chapter discusses advance directives so that you will feel more confident about filling out a living will document, designating a proxy, and/or executing a durable power of attorney for health care declaration. Sample forms are in appendix E. Further information about living wills is available by calling the state agencies listed in appendix F. If you have chosen to fill out an advance directive, you are well on the way to enjoying that peace of mind that comes from knowing that you have done what you can to take care of your needs in the future.

6 · After-Death Planning

Everyone knows death in inevitable. Beyond that, there is little agreement. The concept of death is accompanied by varying interpretations. Some see it as a welcome friend, a natural conclusion to life, or a prelude to rebirth. Others are fearful of death, and see it as punishment, the enemy, or as failure. Some believe that your soul lives on after your body dies; some believe in heaven and hell; some believe in reincarnation. Others believe that once your body dies, that's it—you physical remains are disposed of and it's all over. Some welcome the idea of death but would like it to be later rather than sooner. Some want death right now. Many are comforted by their beliefs, religious or not, and others don't know what they believe and are intrigued by the mystery of it all. Some who feel that life ceases to exist in any form are perfectly comfortable, and others are not. Our attitude toward death and afterlife may well determine the nature of the experience. What do you believe about death and what happens after death?

Preferences

What is your religious affiliation? _____

Name of church, temple, synagogue _____

Name of clergy _____

Clergy telephone number _____

In time of crisis or death, do you want this clergyperson notified? ___

Today four out of five Americans die in hospitals or nursing homes, and, until the hospice movement, family and friends were often separated from the dying person because of various institutional rules. Now the trend returns to dying at home, taking back personal power, and choosing to die the way you would prefer, perhaps in your favorite place, in the midst of loving people with your favorite music in the background. The hospice philosophy focuses on pain relief and enhancing the physical, emotional, and spiritual comfort of the dying person when curing the illness is no longer an option. This enlightened approach includes care for both patients and those caring for them. Check out the hospice care available in you community. Hospice is a philosophy, not a place. Care is primarily implemented in the home, but it can be a special place designated as a hospice or in a hospital or nursing home. Thanks to the hospice philosophy of caring for the whole person, other conventional settings where people are sick and dying appear to be embracing a more holistic approach to dying.

What spiritual/religious practices are important to you?

What are your favorite music, scriptures, hymns, symbols, or prayers?

Death of a loved one is a giant transition time for all involved. Some sort of ritual or service such as a funeral or memorial service helps the survivors say good-bye and begin to face the reality that this person is no longer with them. A service provides an opportunity to express feelings about the deceased and to care for those left behind. It is important that children not feel excluded, that they not be denied the expression of their grief, and that time be taken to answer their questions openly and honestly. Children should be encouraged, but not forced, to participate in the activities. They need to grieve just as adults do if they are going to accept death and not be fearful of it.

When you were a child, was death talked about in your family?
If yes, what was the tone?

What is your earliest memory of someone dying? What do you remember?

Would you prefer to outlive your partner? Why?

How do you speculate that you will die?

For many, there are conditions that seem "worse than death"—times when one's quality of life is deemed no longer acceptable. Discuss the circumstances under which this would apply for you.

Do you consider suicide an option? a sin? something that should be prevented by any means necessary? Discuss. (If you consider suicide a rational option, be sure to discuss this with family members.)

Would you prefer to die at home? at a hospital? with hospice help? How important is this to you? For example, if you prefer to die at home, would you accept transfer to a hospital if it could provide more comfort?

When you die, do you prefer a memorial service? funeral? burial? cremation? reviewal? open casket? closed casket?

Who would you want at your side when you are dying?

Cremation is usually cheaper and simpler because of the need for a less expensive coffin and no embalming or burial costs. It is becoming an increasingly popular choice. You do not need an expensive metal casket if you choose cremation, only a nonmetal alternative container. It is good to think ahead about these matters instead of postponing until you are grieving and under time constraints. There are several choices for what to do with the ashes: special section of cemetery, urn given to family, storage in designated compartment in mausoleum, scattering of ashes in desired location.

If you choose cremation, what do you want done with the ashes?

Some believe in the ritual of an open casket and think that it eases survivors into acceptance of the death. Others disagree, thinking that the added cost of making the deceased "lifelike" isn't worth it. They would prefer to think of the deceased in the vital fullness of life and not see the person dead at all. Still others alternate between the two views, depending on the particular situation and relationship.

What would you prefer?

Another reasonable alternative to a traditional funeral is a memorial society. They are nonprofit, nonsectarian groups that provide modest, respectful funerals at a reasonable cost. By paying a membership fee to the organization, you receive the names of participating funeral directors and help with preplanning.

When planning a funeral, you can obtain the cost of different items over the phone as well as a description and price list of goods and services available. Embalming is not generally required by law, and you have the right to choose cremation or immediate burial if you do not choose embalming.

Where do you want to be buried?

Type of coffin: Softwood ___ Finished hardwood ___
Metal ___ Airtight ___ Leakproof ___
Cheap coffin ("ashes to ashes" occurs quickly) ___
Expense: cheapest ___ more expensive ___ it depends ___

What kind of funeral/memorial/celebration would you like to have?

How important is it to you that your wishes be carried out?
___ "I could care less. When I'm dead, I'm dead, and whatever the survivors want is fine with me."
___ "I feel strongly and would want my wishes carried out."

I would like flowers ___
I would like memorials sent to

_____

_____

There are several ways that you can make things easier on your survivors by preplanning: funeral; will; organ donation; life insurance; and various kinds of trust arrangements (which will be discussed more thoroughly later).

Funerals

Funerals remain the preferred ritual of choice for the majority. Funeral directors report that one-half of the survivors they work with have no notion what kind of funeral the deceased wanted, leaving an unnecessary burden on those left behind. Expenses range dramatically according to the choices you make. It can be helpful to plan your service, make decisions, and perhaps even prepay through various funding vehicles, reducing stress and financial worries for your survivors. Preplanning is always helpful but prepaying can be problematic because persons often move or plans change in some way.

Wills

A will controls the disposition of property at death. In the American Association of Retired Person's *Tomorrow's Choices: Planning for Difficult Times*, financial columnist Jane Bryant Quinn describes a will's function this way: "'You own stuff. You will die. Someone will get your stuff.' If you want to determine who gets your 'stuff' you must have a will. This is true no matter how much or how little money or property you have. Dying without a will—officially called 'intestate'—can create legal headaches and possible conflicts for your survivors. If you do not have a will, the court may determine who gets your possessions."

The state's intestacy laws of "descent and distribution" are impersonal. They cannot choose a guardian for your children, if they are minors, and they cannot make charitable bequests. Joint ownership denies you control over your property while you're living, may not eliminate estate taxes, and may incur gift taxes. So this is a poor substitute for a will. Both husband and wife should have up-to-date wills. If your estate is small, it is still important to have a will because settling takes time and delays usually mean more expense.

State statutes regarding wills vary but most have requirements that a will be signed in the presence of two qualified witnesses and that an executor be named to carry out the provisions of the will. You can change your will by making a new one or adding a "codicil," stating changes to be made. Unofficial alterations will not be effective. The codicil must be written, signed, and witnessed in the same manner as the will and then attached to it. Once your will has been officially executed, sign one copy and keep it in a safe deposit box or ask your attorney to keep it for you. Keep an unsigned duplicate handy so you can check it for updating. If you keep your will in a safe deposit box, you may want a joint owner of the box so that he or she will have easy access to it after your death.

What can you do to reduce attorney fees? Shop comparatively. Also, lawyers charge for their time, so the more organized you are before you arrive, the less the fee. Make a list of what you own, including life insurance, real estate, savings, cars, stocks and bonds, retirement plans, profit sharing, money owed to you, works of art, any meaningful items, and so on. Summarize your wishes for the distribution of your property, listing person's names, addresses, and relationships to you. Name an executor and alternate executor, guardian and alternate guardian for minor children, and any charitable bequests you want to make. Take your Veterans' Administration and social security numbers and your recent income tax records. With the above information in hand, making a will should be an easy task. It is possible but not advisable to write out your own will. I recommend using an attorney's expertise.

Life Insurance

Life insurance is generally purchased to provide a benefit after your death for people who rely on you for financial support. As your dependents become self-supporting and you become financially responsible for only yourself, your life insurance needs decrease. "Whole life" or "universal life" are two types of policies that build a cash value during the life of the insured. Although these policies provide a form of forced savings, the policies may not be competitive with other types of investments. Evaluate your purpose in purchasing insurance and then buy the policy that best accomplishes it. Compare cash value policies with other forms of investments before purchasing a life insurance policy as an investment.

If you need money for current expenses, you might consider surrendering whole life policies for cash or borrowing against your policy. Be very cautious if you decide to convert or change life insurance policies. New policies usually have high up-front costs and often require current evidence of insurability (e.g., health status) that older people may not be able to provide. You might not be able to purchase a new policy at any cost. You should review your life insurance policies every year, and be sure your family members know where you keep the policies. Do not leave them in your safe deposit box. The box may be sealed at your death, causing confusion and delay.

Organ Donation

Improved anti-rejection drugs and surgical procedures have transformed the exotic nature of transplanting organs and tissue to an almost routine event. The first corneal transplant occurred in 1905, the first blood transfusion in 1918, the first kidney transplant in 1954, and the first heart and liver transplants in 1967. Now current medical technology also enables the transplantation of skin, heart, lungs, pancreas, liver, bone, and bone marrow. Today there is a great demand for donor organs. Some organs can come from living donors—kidney, bone marrow, and sometimes liver—but most come from the deceased. The United Network for Organ Sharing in Richmond, Virginia, has about 21,500 patients on its registry waiting for organs. R. L. Worsnop reports that 25 to 30 percent of these are awaiting a liver, heart, or lung and will die before a suitable donor is found.

Organ donation cannot be considered until the donor's whole brain is dead. Once a person is determined to be brain dead, vital organs such as heart or liver need to be oxygenated and supplied with proper chemicals and fluids by artificial means in order for them to remain healthy for transplantation. Other organs such as eyes, bone, skin, and heart valves can be removed several hours after death. The organ donor's health and age are primary factors in whether their organs are fit for transplantation. Vital organs are usually donated by young, healthy person who have died suddenly as the result of an accident. Rarely are people over seventy years of age allowed to donate organs. However, they do often choose to donate their bodies to medical schools for research or their corneas for transplantation. Corneas can be removed up to twenty-four hours after death, regardless of whether the patient is on life support.

The Uniform Anatomical Gift Act of the late 1960s encouraged voluntary donation of organs. Polls indicate that 85 percent of Americans approve of the idea, but very few carry donor cards. Initiatives since then have encouraged organ donation, including the "required request" laws established in the fall of 1990 that require hospitals to inform families of deceased patients of the option to donate organs and tissue. The option to donate an organ, tissue, or your body to science underscores the importance of talking about these issues with your family.

If you want to donate your organs or tissue, send for a donor card. This card becomes a legal document when witnessed and signed by two persons. For information on donor cards, write to:

American Council on Transplantation
700 North Fairfax, Suite 505
Alexandria, VA 22314

Or call 1-800-247-4273. Even with a donor card, or if you have designated "Donor" on you driver's license, your family needs to give permission at the time of death to proceed with organ donation. Do you want to donate your organs or tissue to others in need? Do you wish to donate your body to research?

7 · *Financial and Property Planning*

Another important area where planning for the time when you may be unable or less able to make your own decisions is in the arena of property and financial management. The following is a resource for you when you are seeking information about responsible planning arrangements.

Anyone can be healthy today and incapacitated tomorrow. It is a simple reality that isn't pleasant to think about but needs to be given thought in order to keep your financial affairs in order. Financial considerations are of such overriding concern that basic information to aid in formal and informal planning is included in this book. Major concerns are safeguarding your autonomy, making sure your wishes are known and will be respected regarding financial matters and protecting yourself from the risk of financial exploitation.

Informal Planning

The most important kind of planning can be done with your family members and other people close to you. The average person who has people who know, understand, and agree to comply with his or her wishes will get much of the help needed and will have a relatively easy time with financial planning arrangements. You can find trustworthy persons to write checks, file tax returns, and help you with property management decisions if it becomes difficult for you.

I cannot emphasize enough how important it is to discuss your wishes and plans with others. So often people choose to keep financial matters to themselves; then, when they are no longer able to make decisions or answer clarifying questions, the family discovers for the first time what, if any, arrangements have been made. If a decision-maker has been designated, it makes it far easier for him or her if the whole family knows what arrangements have been made so there is time to answer questions and perhaps negotiate. Problems arise most of the time when family members are puzzled, jealous, or suspicious and don't agree with the arrangements that have been made.

Formal/Legal Planning Tools

Banking Assistance

Modern banking technology has helped persons remain in charge of their finances longer. Persons who are homebound or less able to make financial decisions can ask their banks to arrange automatic bill paying, banking by mail or telephone, and communication via special devices for those with sight or hearing impairments. Direct deposit is available for social security checks and some other pension checks. To arrange for your social security checks to be deposited directly to your bank account, call your local bank or Social Security at 1-800-772-1213 and ask for a direct deposit form.

People sometimes plan ahead by adding another person's name to bank accounts, so that a trusted friend or relative can help by signing checks, paying bills, or transferring money among accounts. There are several different types of multiple-name bank accounts:

Joint account. The other person, considered a co-owner, can make deposits and withdrawals and sign checks. Generally, you should only use joint accounts with your partner or for small accounts. If you do want to set up a joint account with someone other than your partner for over ten thousand dollars, you should first talk with a lawyer about gift tax and income tax laws. Joint accounts can be dangerous. A co-owner could take advantage of you and withdraw all of your money. Or, if he or she has creditors, the creditors could tie up your account with a lien until you could prove how much of the funds you contributed. In addition, sometimes there can be difficulties with Medical Assistance, the program that helps pay nursing home costs, because adding a co-owner to your account is considered to be like giving away property. When you die, in most cases the survivor automatically owns the account, without having to go through probate unless otherwise stated in your will.

Authorized-signer account. The other person can make deposits and withdrawals and sign checks, but does not become an owner of the account. His or her creditors cannot tie up your account, but there is still the risk, as with joint accounts, that the other person could withdraw all your money. The account does not belong to the authorized signer when you die, so the funds in this account belong to your estate.

Payable-on-death account. This account names one or more people to automatically own the account when you die, without having to go through probate. During your lifetime the named person has no right to the account, creditors cannot tie up the account, and he or she cannot make withdrawals or sign checks. This account is not a way to plan ahead for help with finances while you are alive, but rather a way to give your property to loved ones after you die.

Power of Attorney

Simply stated, a power of attorney is a written authorization for someone to handle *property or financial* matters for you, in whatever way you designate, as long as you are alive and able to make decisions. The person signing the power of attorney document is called the principal, and the person named to handle the principal's property is called the attorney-in-fact. The attorney-in-fact does not have to be a lawyer.

A document stating that the attorney-in-fact's power will continue to be valid even if the principal becomes incompetent is called a *durable power of attorney*. This document helps plan the disposition of your matters in the event of future incapacity. After signing a durable power of attorney, you, as the principal, still have the right to control your property as long as you are competent. You can cancel or revoke the power by signing a revocation paper before a notary public. In some states, the durable power of attorney applies more to property matters. In others, it is the main advance directive for health care document (see chapter 6). You must find out what is the most appropriate document; the person to call is your state legal service developer (see appendix F). If the principal becomes incompetent, the power can only be revoked by a guardian or conservator if one is appointed. The principal can entrust limited or broad power to the attorney-in-fact. Be careful to pick a trustworthy person to be your attorney-in-fact and consider naming a successor to take over the responsibility if the first attorney-in-fact dies or becomes incompetent.

Trusts

A trust is a legal arrangement where a person or financial institution, called the trustee, holds legal title and manages assets for the benefit of a person, called the beneficiary. The person who creates and funds the trust is called the grantor. There are two ways a person can create a trust.

Testamentary trust. If the grantor creates the trust in a will to take effect after the grantor dies, it is called a testamentary trust or a death trust because it only activates upon the death of the drafter. A testamentary trust can be an important estate-planning tool, providing for loved ones after the grantor's death. A testamentary trust goes through probate, whereas a living trust can avoid probate.

A living trust. A trust created by a trust agreement during the grantor's lifetime that can be used to plan for incapacity is called a living trust. A trust can be made either revocable or irrevocable. A revocable trust can be changed or terminated by the grantor at any time as long as the grantor is still competent. An irrevocable trust cannot be changed or terminated after it is signed and sealed and the person has basically given up control over the assets that have been placed in the trust. He or she has as income whatever the trust document specifies.

Warning: Salespersons, usually calling themselves estate planners, are selling living trusts to senior citizens, misrepresenting the costs of probate and the tax benefits possible from the trust and falsely promising that trusts will hide or shelter your assets from creditors. They often tell horror stories of probate and are paid on a commission that sometimes exceeds 50 percent of the cost of the product.

Should you use a living trust to plan for incapacity? Living trusts are a very flexible and useful tool for planning for incapacity, but because of their cost, trusts are most advantageous for estates over six hundred thousand dollars because at that point you can take advantage of the federal estate tax exemption. There are legal fees for setting up the trust agreement, plus handling fees. Institutional trustees usually will not accept a trust unless it has at least fifty to one hundred thousand dollars in assets because the expense of maintaining the trust would be too great. A family member or other individual could be named trustee, but some degree of expertise is necessary to handle the paperwork, tax returns, and property management tasks that may be involved.

One way to use a living trust to plan for incapacity is to set up the trust, but not put any or much money or property into it. Then sign a durable power of attorney, instructing your attorney-in-fact to transfer your money and property to the trust only if you do become incompetent or incapacitated. This type of arrangement is often called a "standby trust."

What is probate? When you die, your property needs to be distributed. Probate is a legal process for transferring your property to your heirs. Probate varies from state to state, but in general:

1. An executor is named to handle the affairs of the estate. The executor may be designated in the will of the deceased, or if there is no will, designated by the probate judge.

2. Creditors of the deceased are given two to nine or more months to determine liabilities.

3. The estate is appraised and everything is assigned a value.

4. Federal estate taxes must be paid.

5. Anyone can contest the will through probate court.

Many people fear the expense and delay of probate. Probate does take time. Seek legal advice for ways to safeguard your heirs from having to go through this process.

Should you use a living trust to avoid probate? Perhaps, but there are other choices. If a married couple owns all their property jointly, there is usually no need for probate when one dies; all the property will automatically belong to the survivor. The same is true for life insurance proceeds; they automatically go to the named beneficiary without probate. To make sure that your property is passed on according to your wishes in the safest, fastest, least expensive way possible, you should get qualified legal advice.

Living trusts generally help avoid probate costs and permit your assets to be distributed more quickly after death. They are definitely worth investigating. For some, living trusts are appropriate, but not for all. Beware of scare tactics and do not be afraid to shop comparatively. Lawyers can give you estimates of their fees for setting up a trust, and you can get estimates of trustee fees from the persons or institutions that you are considering naming as trustee. Often it costs more in legal fees to draft a trust than a will, and you or your heirs pay annual fees to the managing institution.

Should you use a living trust to avoid paying nursing home costs? Some people try to use living trusts as a way to qualify for medical assistance to avoid spending their savings on nursing home care. This can be very risky and can backfire. The medical assistance rules are very complicated and are subject to change at any time. Do not try to use a trust for this purpose without getting competent legal advice.

Conservatorship Planning

What are guardianship and conservatorship? Guardianship and conservatorship are legal processes to protect persons who are incapacitated and cannot handle their own financial or personal decisions. The responsibilities of the two processes vary from state to state, so should be checked, but in general they are similar, except that guardianship takes away more civil rights, such as the right to vote. For this reason, conservatorship is used more frequently than guardianship. The protected person is called the conservatee, and the person named by the court to make decisions is called the conservator. If a person becomes incapacitated, unable to handle finances, and did not previously make any planning arrangements, a conservatorship may be the only way to pay the bills and handle the person's property. Anyone can petition to be the person's conservator, and a conservator may be appointed whether or not the incapacitated person wants one. However, if you plan ahead, you can protect your independence, even if a time comes when you need a conservator, by doing conservatorship planning.

What is conservatorship planning? Conservatorship planning is a written document, witnessed in the same way as a will, where you can name the person you would want for your conservator and give instructions on how you would want your personal and financial matters handled. For example, the conservator could be instructed on how to manage your property, where you would like to live, and be privy to your wishes regarding health care. Then, at a later date, if you become incapacitated and need a conservator, the court must name your chosen conservator and order that your instructions be followed, unless the court finds that this would not be in your best interests.

Do I need to do conservatorship planning if I already have made informal planning arrangements with relatives or formal arrangements such as an advance directive? Everyone's situation is different. If you have other informal or formal planning arrangements, you may not need to do conservatorship planning. However, if it is likely that someone would challenge your planning arrangements or that your family will disagree among themselves, you would be well advised to use conservatorship planning as a back-up to your other planning arrangements. Anyone can petition for conservatorship for an incapacitated person, and a conservator can revoke or terminate prior planning arrangements.

By naming your own conservator, you have the best possible legal protection against the appointment of someone you do not want to be your conservator. It is when there is tension and disagreement in your family that you know about now, or suspect could flare up, that it becomes imperative to ensure that you have planned for all contingencies. Conservatorship planning not only covers management of property but personal planning as well. You can state your wishes about financial and property planning in addition to your health-care planning preferences, whether you are terminally ill or not. Conservatorship planning is the most foolproof way of guaranteeing that your wishes are respected.

8 · *Housing Options and Services*

Another area of information gathering necessary for responsible planning is to review the numerous housing options that are available for older adults and the increasing number of services that are making it easier for persons to remain in their own homes. This chapter briefly describes the options and services that provide you with choices. Also, the National Eldercare Locator Line, 1-800-677-1116, will link you with the service providers in your area. Have the zip code of the area you want to know about handy.

Stay at Home

There is a full range of health-care and social services for persons of any age who need assistance and choose to continue living in their own homes. Bringing services into your home helps relieve stress for the caregiver and can greatly enhance overall quality of life. Some of the services are listed below.

Emergency response systems. Electronic monitors are available that activate an attachment on your telephone that is tied into the emergency room of the hospital, police department, or emergency squad. It allows older adults to live alone but never be out of contact with help in case of an emergency. The older adult who lives alone wears or carries in a pocket a small wireless help button that, when pushed, calls an emergency number. When the call comes in, a trained listener immediately calls the sender to see what the problem is and then, if the sender does not answer, calls one of the designated responders, who could be a neighbor or a family member, to go to the home immediately. It is an inexpensive service, and one that stretches the freedom of the person living alone.

Friendly visiting/peer counseling. Volunteers working under the umbrella of senior service organizations, hospitals, churches, and synagogues listen, do errands, write letters, and provide companionship.

Meals on Wheels. Volunteers bring one hot meal a day to the homebound. Fees vary.

Home health-care agencies. Home health-care agencies provide a spectrum of care from occupational and physical therapy and homemaker services to advanced skilled nursing services with mobile technology such as ventilators and oxygen. Medicaid often covers home health care. The degree to which private insurance cover these services varies widely. Check the yellow pages or your local Area Agency on Aging for information.

Homemakers/aides. Aides do light housekeeping and assist in personal care such as bathing and dressing. Sometimes, if under supervision, they can monitor medication.

Chore service helpers. Helpers clean, shop, wash clothes, cook, and sometimes make small repairs in the house and do yardwork.

Note: There is a confusion or overlap in the definition of homemakers/aides, chore services, home health care, home improvement, and personal care services. Different parts of the country label the helper categories differently. When asking the Area Agency on Aging for information, specify the tasks that need to be done and they will be able to tell you the service category.

Transportation services. Transportation services vary from community to community. Many have reduced fares for seniors on public transportation, medical vehicles from hospitals, nonmedical transports for medical appointments (e.g., American Cancer Society), senior center buses, and special taxi rates. Learn how to access these services. Call the Area Agency on Aging for information and referral numbers in your community. Obtain a resource directory for your area. Order a silver pages telephone directory by calling 1-800-252-6060. Use yellow pages to find transportation, nutrition services, home health care, societies for persons with vision or hearing impairments, and local senior centers.

Delivery services. Dry cleaners, food markets, catalogue retailers, and pharmacies that deliver are springing up. Cable television offers shop-at-home services.

Escort services. Volunteer and paid escort services are available in some communities.

Libraries. Libraries offer special services to the homebound. Books can be delivered or mailed along with "talking books" services. Call your local library or national office at 1-800-424-8567.

Adult day care. Adult day care provides social and rehabilitative activities to older adults during the day in a community facility. Participants can attend one to five days a week. It is often a perfect solution for all involved in situations where adult children or a spouse who works during the day or needs relief from caregiving responsibilities at home can have a safe, stimulating place for a loved one during the day.

Legal assistance. Legal assistance may be available for those who need help with wills, taxes, public program benefits, protection services, disability care. Inquire through Lawyer Information and Referral Services, Legal Aid Society, or Legal Counsel for the Elderly (look in your Yellow Pages).

Mental health services. Mental health services for addiction and abuse problems as well as everyday life transitions and adjustment to loss are available through community mental health agencies and sometimes through senior service agencies and senior centers.

Respite care for caregivers. Respite care is available in some communities. This service allows persons who care for another in their home full-time to get some rest and re-energize.

Telephone reassurance or communicare. Telephone reassurance is a program available in some communities where homebound elderly are called (or may call in) daily by a volunteer to assure that all is well.

Hospices. Hospices operate under the philosophy that persons at the end of their lives should be made as comfortable as possible and given every opportunity in the remaining time to live life as fully as possible. Home hospice help is available in homes as well as in the hospital and some nursing homes. When "cure" is no longer possible, "care" and comfort become the focus.

"Golden Age" banking services. These banking services offer a discounted brokerage service, direct deposit of social security checks, free traveler's checks, no service charge, and/or payment of utility bills as inducements for older adults.

Case management. Case management involves individuals who assess the needs of an individual and match him or her with services.

Congregate dining. Congregate dining offers nutritionally balanced meals to older people in a social setting such as a senior center, church, or school. A donation is requested but the meals are subsidized.

Weatherization and fuel assistance. Federal and state aid, which varies from state to state, are available to low-income households for weatherization and fuel assistance, sometimes including free energy audits, insulation, and the cost of labor.

Housing Options

Often older adults begin to "think smaller." They begin to think that they don't need as much room, as much upkeep, or as much expense and start looking at various options.

Accessory apartments. One converts an area of one's house into an apartment for a family member and/or rents it out for additional income or moves into it and rents the bulk of the house.

Share-a-home. For reduced rent, an older person with a home shares it with another person who helps with household chores.

Reverse mortgage/home equity. Home equity allows older persons to remain in their own homes and receive set payments from their home's equity for a predetermined number of years. Basically, it means selling your house but continuing to live in it. It allows you to convert your home equity to liquid assets, enabling you to continue living there. Check out the variations in your area. Write to:

National Center for Home Equity Conversions
110 E. Main, Room 1010
Madison, Wisconsin 53703

Condominiums. Individually owned units in a complex where common property is jointly owned. This is often a first step for healthy, independent older adults who no longer want a large home, want less maintenance responsibility, and want more security.

Cooperatives. These are multi-unit developments where residents own shares in the whole enterprise versus owning individual units.

Senior citizen apartment communities. These feature private living quarters but easy access to transportation, social activities, dining, and housekeeping services. Sometimes a meal a day is included in the monthly fee. Congregate housing is rental housing with services.

Rental housing. This includes single family homes, apartments, and town houses. Costs range from government-subsidized to expensive.

Adult care homes. Sometimes called foster homes, these generally provide meals and personal care and some degree of supervision in a private home. They are not considered medical facilities but medical help is available. Boarding homes tend to serve a particular category of residents—older persons and those with mental retardation or physical disabilities. They provide room, board, and personal assistance.

Life care communities or continuing care retirement communities (CCRCs). These types of communities provide a full range of services from apartments for independent living to skilled nursing care. They generally require monthly payments plus an entrance fee that is sometimes refundable at death. Life care communities are usually more expensive than others, but prices and contractual agreements vary widely. Some are luxury high-rises with communal living resembling fancy restaurants; others look more like college dining halls, serving cafeteria-style meals.

Nursing homes/retirement centers. Nursing homes and retirement centers provide twenty-four-hour access to skilled care or intermediate custodial care. Medicare pays only for skilled and acute care. It does not pay for care for chronic illnesses such as Alzheimer's or bedridden stroke victims. Quality homes often have waiting lists. It is smart and responsible to investigate the homes in your area and put yourself on a waiting list. You are under no obligation to go into the facility when your name rises to the top of the list, but it is wonderful insurance to know the option is available when you're ready. As far away as this prospect might seem, it is sound planning to do this early and remove this worry from your mind. Nursing homes can be the best alternative for many reasons:

- if you need more medical attention than you can receive elsewhere
- if you need short-term care after a hospital stay
- if you worry about being a burden to your family or your caregiver(s) is wearing down
- if you require so much nursing care in your home that the costs exceed your ability to pay
- if you feel isolated in your own house and choose to have more sociability (if this is the only reason, there are probably other alternatives)

This chapter enumerates some of the vast number of housing options and services available for older adults. Not all of them will be obtainable in your area, but, if you inquire, you might be surprised at how many are. Knowing what your options are empowers you. Even if you don't choose to use any of the options or services, knowing that they're available is comforting. Please give some thought to what you might want for yourself in the future.

Conclusion

Part 2, "This Is My Responsibility," has given you information about your options and the opportunity to reflect upon this knowledge with your own unique preferences and values in mind. The purpose is to aid you in planning in the areas of health care, finance, housing, and services. What fits best for you? You now have the information needed to assist you in making plans congruent with your values and your dreams. Plans and decisions for your future that you have made are a major ingredient in attaining peace of mind.

Whatever you can do,
or dream you can,
begin it.
Boldness has genius,
power and magic in it.
—Goethe

Part 3 Self-Renewal: This Is How I Want to Live the Rest of My Life

Part 1 of this book, "This Is Who I Am," helped you to become reacquainted with yourself. By pulling together the many components of your own unique story, recognizing its complexities, looking at your sad times as well as your joyful memories, and identifying your admirable and strong qualities, you have the context for integrating these many parts and planning for your future.

Part 2, "This Is My Responsibility," helped you sort your values and priorities about late-life issues and gave you enough information to allow you to make concrete plans. If you have already filled out the advance directives provided you may have discovered how empowering it is to be responsible for and take charge of your future.

There are, however, many things in life that you can't control: natural disasters such as hurricanes and floods, your genetics, your predisposition to illness, what other people do, and the undeniable fact that your physical body will die one day.

You are not going to get out of this life alive. But you can do much to make this life "alive" while you are here.

This section, "Self-Renewal," is about how to live. It is a how-to primer on ways to make your life as full and meaningful as possible. It gives you information and suggestions on how to renew yourself using three approaches: discovering and appreciating the meaningfulness of your life; learning specific skills of self-care; and enhancing your attitude. What does it mean to live life fully and meaningfully? One thing it does not mean is that you will be problem-free or without some pain. In fact, one of the criteria for enlightenment and living life fully is to accept the inevitability and cyclical nature of grief. If you love and care about anyone or anything, you are guaranteed a certain amount of pain. This fact places people in a quandary throughout life. You toddle along measuring your thoughts, saying to yourself, "I shouldn't get into this relationship or take a risk like this. I'll get hurt." Yet it is when you start overprotecting yourself from hurt and back away from caring that you lose the joy of truly living.

Caring often gives you pain and, ironically, caring is also the best way to heal. Living fully means keeping your heart open. Healing is choosing to move toward love and kindness versus closing yourself off and resisting life. Dwelling on missed opportunities, bad choices, and poor relationships blocks any movement toward peace of mind. The point at which you stop resisting and trying to control a situation is when healing begins to occur. It is when you stop fighting the past and learn to let go that extraordinary growth and completion can occur. Though this often happens at the end of life, some discover the secret much earlier.

This section discusses feelings—what to do with your own, how to react to others', and how to ask for what you want. You will find suggestions on how to thrive in the present and how to develop the best possible attitude toward your remaining time so that you can live richly with its uncertainty and mystery. The section gives suggestions for letting go of those weights of the past that may be still draining your energy.

> *The afternoon of life must also have a significance of its own and cannot be merely an appendage to life's morning.*
> —Carl Jung

You are encouraged to lean back and marvel at all you have learned. If you paused to look at your past in part 1, recalling your many experiences, you are now better able to see your individual experiences as part of a whole.

Life is a process. It is always changing and you continue learning as you move through it. In *The Will to Meaning*, Victor Frankl says that life is full of meaning that you can discover and learn great lessons from if you study your life patterns. Frankl says, "Remember what I have said about life's transitoriness. In the past nothing is irrevocably lost but everything is irrevocably stored. People only see the transitoriness but overlook the full granaries of the past in which they have been delivered and deposited, in which they have been saved, their harvest."

When you find what is good for you and hold fast to it, you become whole.
—Author Unknown

You have questions, fantasies, dreams, and hopes and they change and are moderated all the time. You may have fantasized the man in your life to be tall and muscular and then found yourself with a not-so-tall and not-so-muscular fellow who seems just about right. You may have fantasized about yourself or a child of yours as a major league athlete and it didn't happen. You may have been terrified of growing older since society paints old age so grimly and now find aging quite liberating and satisfying. You may have thought you would live into old age with the person you married, but it hasn't worked out that way because of divorce or death. You are forced to set aside the old dreams, readjust, and go on. Journeys are like this. Questions change. Realities change. Just when you are halfway there, you discover that the goal has changed. With new experiences, your world becomes different. Wonderful things happen and tragedies happen and you are never the same as before. Life is about changing and adapting.

It is never too late and never too soon to change.

9 · Meaning

Most older adults yearn for a life that has mattered and continues to matter. They know by now that it is not money, acquisitions, or power that satiates this hunger. It is when life has meaning that people feel purposeful and happy. Happiness is a by-product, not a goal. One way to move toward closing your circle of wholeness is to determine what gives your own life meaning. This chapter is intended as a catalyst for insight, providing a framework for discovering the meaning in your life. If you have taken time to journey with yourself through these pages, you now have a better idea of what has been most important to you, a greater appreciation of the complex richness of life, and a good start toward attributing meaning to life's lessons. Life is like a good book—the more you get into it, the more things start to fall into place. Perhaps you will be able to see not only the uniqueness of your journey, but also see how your journey connects with others.

The marks left by one individual on another are eternal.
—François Mauriac, *A Christmas Tale*

You probably cannot find ultimate meaning. You can, however, find little clarifying meanings that move you in the direction of ultimate meaning. It is the search that provides true meaning. You don't automatically become wise as you age. In fact, some never become wise. The inflexible ones actually choose not to change. Experience can, but does not necessarily, bring wisdom; it is what you learn from your experiences that brings wisdom. Additional years of experience offer possibilities for clarity about previously incomprehensible wonderments and a better chance of seeing how your own journey fits into the bigger picture. This can happen only if you are open to it.

When the student is ready, the teacher will appear.
—Native American Saying

When students are receptive, they will learn and gain wisdom. The person you are today is an accumulation of your experiences, and what you have learned guides not only your own future but the lives of those around you. Information moves from one person to another. Those who are enlightened spread their light to others.

I honor the place in you
where the entire universe resides.
I honor the place in you
of love, of light, of peace.
I honor the place within you where,
if you are in that place in you,
and I am in that place in me,
there is only one of us.
—Nameste (an East Indian prayer and greeting)

A long life provides many opportunities to discover beauty, to pause and to wonder. Time becomes more precious and an ever greater gift. Who has led a perfect life? The fact is, having to survive imperfections and losses helps you discover the depth of your being. When you are living the lows, it is hard to embrace the notion that it is a learning experience. Still, most of the time you do learn and change. Change is an exciting constant and forces your reality, your goals and dreams, to be altered. In *The Measure of My Days*, Florida Scott-Maxwell describes the mystery and intrigue of aging: "A long life makes me feel nearer truth, yet it won't go into words, so how can I convey it? I can't and I want to. I want to tell people approaching and perhaps fearing age that it is a time of discovery. If they say 'Of what?' I can only answer, 'We must each find out for ourselves, otherwise it won't be a discovery.' "

Discover your own meaning!

Clarifying Questions

If you were asked by a child to tell about the most important thing you have learned in your life, what would you say?

What was the best period of your life? Why?

What was the worst time of your life? Why? Did you know it at the time? What did you learn?

If you could write the service for your funeral, what would you say?

What do you think was the best thing you ever did for someone else?

If you could have anything in the world, what would it be?

If you could give anything in the world to someone else, what would you give? To whom?

What projects have given you the most pleasure?

What have you worked hardest at (work, social causes, friendships, marriage, parenting)?

For what do you want to be remembered?

Once you answer these questions for yourself, you will be able to articulate what is most fulfilling for you. Your next move toward self-renewal is to make time to do more of the things that make you feel joyful and full of life. You can find answers to many of life's perplexing decisions by asking yourself: What response or action can I take that will make me like myself the most?

Most people's souls are hungry for purpose, for meaning, for knowing that somehow they have made and are making a difference to someone or something. A sense of purpose does not mean you have to save the world or think in lofty terms about meaningfulness. Being kind and caring to one other person is purpose. The important thing is for you to rearrange your thinking to acknowledge to yourself that you do have a purpose for being here. Not being able to label a purpose leads people into depression and despair. Those persons who have a goal, a project, or exude purposefulness are living their lives fully whether or not their physical body is cooperating.

Nobody grows old by living a number of years.
People grow old from lack of purpose.
Years wrinkle the skin.
Lack of purpose wrinkles the soul.
　—Author Unknown

You know people who let their ailing bodies and illnesses dominate their every moment. Nothing else seems to exist for them. On the other hand, two women, ages eighty and eighty-one, with whom I was visiting recently, were so wrapped up in world issues, so full of vigor and enthusiasm, that only in passing did their annoyance with their physical problems emerge. One had had cancer for seventeen years, had recently had a pump installed to directly inject chemicals into her liver, and seemed to pay little attention to the subject except to mutter, "What a bother it all is." The other, also in passing, laughed at how she has to strap her head into some sort of traction contraption every morning, worrying that someone could burst into her apartment and think that she is hanging herself.

Why is an illness for one person so preoccupying and for another merely a bother, an annoyance? Could it be that, even though these women are interested and methodically take care of their bodies as best they can, their major interests and curiosities lie outside themselves? Or is it because they just don't have the accompanying pain that preoccupies others? Perhaps, but even persons who have considerable pain choose how they react to it. It appears that in order to see life as meaningful, you need to have a purpose and to care beyond yourself.

A young man said to a very old man,
"What is your greatest burden as you grow old?"
The ancient one replied,
"That I have nothing to carry."
　—Asian Saying

So many older adults waste their last valuable years, the time of mature perspective and potential spiritual vision. When retirees, or anyone whose role has changed, are no longer focused on career, they often flounder, some for the first time, and wonder about their identity, asking, "Who am I now? Why should I get up on Monday?" All their lives people say that they want choices, but not having their life organized as they did for years with work or children, and not knowing precisely what they are going to do on this day presents a major dilemma. When your role changes, you have a time management problem and perhaps too many choices on your hands. This is not because you are suddenly a different person. Who you are and what is important in life is rooted in something far more basic than what your job or role was. Even though you are always changing, and conditions around you change, the basic substance you are made of is constant. You can choose to keep those parts of your personality that you like. You can also determine something satisfying to do now, perhaps something that makes a contribution. Let your curiosity lead you. You have nothing to lose and much to gain by trying out a "new and improved you."

This is a time of great opportunity. What new things do you want to try? Many don't look at that question. They feel forced into idleness and appear to accept the societal standard that the best time of life is over and it is now time to wither on the vine. Not so! Sometimes it is helpful to think of this time of life as you look at vacations. What shall I do today? What activities would make you feel good about yourself? It is time to do some of those things you regret not having done earlier. If you regret not "being there" enough as a parent, perhaps you can spend more time with your grandchildren. Maybe it is a time to attend to friendships that you have let slide. Here are examples of ways some older adults have chosen to make their lives meaningful:

Continue learning. Take classes, attend Elderhostels, go to college or graduate school. Agnes got her Ph.D. in American history at age ninety-two from the Union Institute.

Follow your curiosities. Try traveling, pottery making, jewelry making, quilting, painting, working with stained glass, trying new recipes, embroidering, singing, dancing, sewing, woodworking. Billy was caning chairs at the age of eighty-eight.

Volunteer. Volunteer for your church, schools, clubs, hospices, hospitals. Phyllis, age eighty-nine, visits the "old folks" in the nursing home every Wednesday.

Investigate family history, write journals, create photo albums, shift family films to videos. At age seventy-five, Bill traveled to Norway to do family tree research.

Teach others your skills. Joe, a retired banker, helps people manage their money volunteering at a bank and high school at age eighty-three.

Care for children or someone in need, visit and do errands for people who need help, make phone calls to people who are homebound and need to know someone is interested, deliver Meals on Wheels. After retirement, Dave spends three hours each week recording books on tape for the blind.

Find new hobbies. Take up fishing, golfing, antiques collecting, bird watching, gardening, golfing. Helen became an avid bowler in her seventies.

Find a new job, a new career. Bob, a retired dentist, works as a sales-man at a major discount store.

Do something about what you believe in passionately. Esther started lobbying the legislature on gun control at age seventy-eight.

Help others. Join the Peace Corps, work with Jimmy and Rosalynn Carter's Habitat for Humanity, use your insights and become involved in causes that are concerns of all age groups (such as domestic violence and helping your planet survive). Commit random acts of kindness and senseless acts of beauty. Create meaning by prac-ticing guerrilla goodness. Say hello. Be friendly to your neighbors or to strangers. Take a hot dish to someone. Send flowers anonymously. Write some friendly notes to people. Fix someone a dinner by candle-light.

Be silly or bizarre. Clean your house in the nude. Sleep in your yard under the stars. Do "love" as an activity. Think of ways to express your caring. Listen to another. Encourage someone to be all they can be.

Besides the obvious psychological and spiritual benefits of doing good, it is now well established that there is a physical pay-off for you, the helper. Allan Luks and Peggy Payne in *The Healing Power of Doing Good* report that helping others gives the helper a "helper's high." A "helpers high involves physical sensations that strongly indicate a sharp reduction in stress and a release of the body's natural pain killers, the endorphins. This initial rush is followed by a longer-lasting period of improved emotional well-being." So what you have always known has now been proven clinically; when you focus on things outside yourself there is actual physical relief from aches and pains.

You can do your part to change the negative stereotypes of older adults by modeling living a full and life-affirming existence, by being a person who enjoys the benefits your stage of life brings. If you model the empowerment and liberation that can come with later life by continuing to learn, risk, care about things, and be joyous, the outdated image will change.

Differences Between Middle-aged and Older Adults

> *I am far better able to cope at 70 than at 50.*
> *I think that is partly because I have learned to glide*
> *instead of to force myself at moments of tension.*
> —May Sarton, *At Seventy*

One of the important lessons of life is to learn to glide, to go with the flow, and learn to enjoy the journey itself. The societal value of always seeking a goal or destination often obscures the importance of giving day-to-day events depth and value and causes people, especially in harried mid-life, to let little enjoyments go by unnoticed. This lesson of appreciating the moment has to be learned and relearned and older people have a special advantage in finally "getting it" because they have had more practice. They have a perspective attainable only through years of experience. Not only that, but their awareness of their own mortality makes them more likely to take the time to appreciate the view.

You are different when you are older. Some things are better; some things are worse. Unfortunately, society encourages you to continue to accept middle-age standards instead of embracing the values of later life:

View from Middle Age	View from Later Life
Attitude of "more is better"	Enough is enough
External accomplishments valued	Inner work more important
Control/independence of major importance	Control/independence still important but balanced with freeing ability to "let go"
Do what you "have to"	Do what you want to
Focus on self and/or immediate world (work, children, family, friends)	See self as part of greater whole

Facade necessary to present best self, to "fit in"	Time to be real, free to be yourself
Important to look confident	Okay to feel humble, without answers
Society sets your agenda: need to produce, earn money, perform	You set your own agenda
Time to be serious, responsible	Time to reclaim sense of awe, lightheartedness
Look for "answers," assuredness	Tolerate ambiguity, uncertainty, affirm importance of questions
Worried about future	Can focus on present, live more spontaneously
Feel immortal (even though you know you are not)	Belief in own mortality brings greater appreciation of living
Feel stressed, fatigued	Nap a lot
Feel negative and fearful about old age	Realistic—know that old age can be anything
Problems are "making it," getting ahead, surviving	Problems are adjusting to losses such as loved ones who die and own health
Parenting is full time	Enjoy the good stuff about grand children, then send them home
No safety net for health-care or financial emergency	Medicare and social security
Emphasis on "doing"	Easier to just "be" with no definable "doer" role

None of this is clear-cut. First of all, there is no clear dividing line between middle age and old age. Old age is not an entity unto itself; it is a stage of development. Second, the distinctions are only generalizations leading to the following point: *In order to find life meaningful, it is important for older people to believe that their later years are as valuable as their earlier years.*

This is not about right and wrong nor finding fault with other stages. It is not wrong to value productivity and consumption when you are supporting a family any more than it is wrong to luxuriate in the liberation from the pressure of having to prove yourself. There are not two sides to this. It is necessary for a younger person to learn how to be independent, to be responsible and take care of herself or himself. You cannot learn the value of healthy interdependence unless you have learned to be independent at an earlier developmental stage. Persons who are older adults today were productivity oriented and proponents of competition when younger. Now they are pointing the way, showing mid-lifers what their future selves may be doing and thinking. In the final analysis, this is really about one person struggling with the different stages in his or her life and being in partnership with these different parts.

It is important to affirm this later stage of life and encourage the accompanying ways of thinking that promote self-appreciation. One major hindrance to positive aging is continuing to equate only paid work with self-worth and diminishing the value of worthy avocations such as reading, traveling, volunteering, and caregiving. Life is likely to become meaningless and empty for those who can't expand their thinking about what constitutes basic self-worth. It is time to attribute new, positive meaning to getting older and stop tolerating the deeply ingrained societal adoration of youth and negativity toward age. All stages of life have merit and problems. The stress of supporting yourself and/or family during middle age is a problem as is adjusting to losses of various sorts in later life. The important thing to note is that "being old" itself isn't the problem. Do not acquiesce to this notion. This time of life is loaded with opportunities for meaning-making and satisfaction.

What is meant by meaning-making? An easy way to begin understanding what is meaningful is to recall for yourself times that you would consider to be peak moments.

Peak Moments

"Peak moments" are those precious times when you know that "life doesn't get any better than this," moments when you stand in awe of nature or a work of art, when you know that you've truly connected with another person, when you have achieved a personal victory, or when you have completed a job "well done." For some of you, peak moments may occur when you feel fully known, accepted, and loved by another or when you give and receive love simultaneously. They may have occurred in the moment when you witnessed your child being born, when you caught that enormous fish, when you viewed a waterfall or a rainbow, or when you felt safe enough to have challenged someone and come out of the encounter feeling proud of yourself. Perhaps the moment occurred during the simple exchange of a supportive glance, when water caressed your body as you swam, when you heard rain on the roof of a tent, when you nursed your baby and it looked up at you and smiled, when you ran through a meadow with the wind in your hair, or when you snuggled close to the warmth of a person you love. They are the times when you've felt feelings of awe, reverence, tenderness, or pride.

These moments can't be taken from you. They are timeless events; points where measured time touches eternity. After someone close to you dies, certain memories become peak moments and are immortalized. Those meaning-filled moments suspend your sense of time. Recently, I was putting Vicks on my granddaughter's chest. At that moment I had a sense that, besides being a grandmother, I was my mother, and I was myself as a child. It felt comfortable, complex, and eternal.

List some of your peak moments of the past and look for them daily. These are the "little meanings" that start to add up.

Peak Moments

Sweet glimpses of holiness . . .
nothing can be better than this!
I am alive.

What makes you feel most alive?

"Follow your bliss" says Joseph Campbell in *The Power of Myth.* What does this mean?

Bliss is the way we experience the connection
between our individual consciousness
and the larger consciousness beyond human knowing.
—William Blake

"Follow your bliss" speaks to taking action versus simply appreciating little bursts of bliss should they occur. Following your bliss requires you to actively pursue those moments. Once you recognize what it is that makes you feel vibrantly alive, you can then use this awareness as a source of guidance in your life. When you give love, there is often a sense of timelessness, a sense of giving that does not require reciprocity, and a clean sense of purity that lets you know you are much more than yourself; you are connected to everyone, everything. Peak experiences may be moments of earthly, heartwarming pleasure but they are also eternal. They are the fleeting moments in which you witness your own being and understand the purpose in life, even though you may not be able to articulate that knowing. They cannot be taken away from you.

You cannot stay on the summit forever;
you have to come down again.
So why bother in the first place?
Just this: what is above knows what is below,
but what is below does not know what is above.
One climbs, one sees, one descends;
one sees no longer, but one has seen.
When one can no longer see,
one can at least still know.
We live by what we have seen.
    —Rene Daumal, *Mount Analogue*

If you know what your bliss is, then you often can direct your journey. Many students can get through the required amount of hoop-jumping only by knowing they will be able to contribute in a way that will give life meaning in the long run. While on a long-dreamed-about canoe trip on the Missinabi River in Ontario, I distinctly remember nine miles of portaging through muddy muck and an army of mosquitoes. With a canoe on my shoulders and salty sweat in my eyes, I lost my foothold trying to negotiate a slippery log in a swampy area. As I sank into the muck, I started giggling to myself and muttering, "I'm following my bliss; I'm following my bliss." To actively follow one's bliss is not always easy, but when it is your choice, the agonies are transformed to sweet hurts like the physical weariness you feel after strenuous exercise.

As you age, you often need to find creative new ways to follow your bliss. I found that beating a drum has the same satisfying effect on my soul as did slamming a racquetball in earlier years, along with some additional joys and benefits. Wheelchair-bound or bedridden older adults find new, substitute pleasures to allow them to continue following their bliss. Bliss is not necessarily an activity. It can be simply enjoying the moment or caring for another. Many professional and family caregivers experience bliss with the satisfying awareness that they are doing "whatever can be done" for someone they care about and love. Even the pangs of grief and loneliness after a major loss are compensated for by the awareness that you would not trade those present feelings for never having loved at all.

Exquisite grief . . .
Exquisite living . . .
Bliss.

Practice Simplicity

Make special note of the simple things that give you pleasure and set a goal to learn to live each moment, to savor the ordinary, so that life contains more and more of these holy moments. You can learn to make even trivial-seeming acts luminous and vital: making tea, looking at the stars, taking a bath, feeling the warm sun on your back. Notice every detail.

In character
in manners
in style
in all things
the supreme excellence
is simplicity.
   —Henry Wadsworth Longfellow

Why is it when you are in the middle of life you don't or can't take time to appreciate the splendor of what's going on? When my children were little, I can remember pausing long enough as I raced through a room to ponder why my mother took such pure, unadulterated joy in playing with her grandchildren, chuckling and thoroughly appreciating all of their remarks. I was at least aware enough to acknowledge to myself that "she probably knows what life's all about." Then, I went on my hurried way. Now I'm there myself. and I marvel at my grandchildren. I choose to take the time and know that the simplest things are, indeed, the most profound.

When my mother, much later in life and in the middle stages of Alzheimer's, didn't know where she was, didn't know my name, didn't know or care what was going on in the world, she still could marvel at the "leaves wiggling on the trees," the squirrels dashing about, could ooh and ahh at a baby placed in her arms. Was she still teaching me that basic lesson about the simplicity and profoundness of life?

Developmentally, we appear to move from the simple awe and curiosity in a child's face to complexity as a middle-aged "fast track" person and back to a very appreciative simplicity again. This late life appreciation is much more sophisticated and hopeful because we have experienced much of what life has to offer and now choose to attribute meaning to the simple things with a deeper perception of their enormous value.

What Makes the Ordinary Extraordinary?

In a flower, in the sea, in the forest, in a kind glance—there is pleasure. Memories of those Sunday evenings spent as a child with my family listening to favorite radio shows, playing gin rummy or cribbage, eating popcorn somehow have made the magic switch in my memory from being ordinary and even boring at the time to being extraordinary.

What follows is a note I received from a dear friend around her ninetieth birthday.

Dear Trish,

Thank you for your note and family picture. I so treasure the update. You asked me how I am. Quite well I think. It strikes me as funny that I say I feel so well when to look at me you might wonder. I have gotten quite unsteady on my feet, my hearing is so bad that I have my TV blasting so that the kids laugh when they come to visit. My cancer is still with me but being decently managed and relatively peaceful at present. So being able to say "quite well" takes on an amazing slant. No one could have made me believe that I—the real me—who, even though it definitely includes my body, am obviously much more than just that, could have adjusted to life's maladies and truly feel quite serene and pleased with myself.

I was thinking last week how I used to wonder with alarm about how my mother occupied her time after my father died. Even though she didn't complain, I couldn't figure what she did all day and suffered for her boring, lonely-seeming life. I encouraged her to move in with Elizabeth or Lucy, two of her many widowed friends who lived alone in their relatively big houses. She said to me then and I remember thinking that this was, perhaps, wisdom—"I want to live alone. I am not lonely. I know that you can't understand this because you are at a time of life when you need people around. I felt the same at your age. Now I prefer being alone, doing what I want to do when I want to do it."

I'm now older than she was when she said that to me. I think of it often and I do understand it, dear mother. Life evolves in such an interesting way. Getting old isn't better or worse than being young; it is just different. I seem to be entertained by the very simple. I love watching the birds at the feeder and the squirrels scampering around. I love listening to my new music system. Mary gave me a fancy CD player that makes me feel like I'm sitting in an orchestra pit. I love my oatmeal and brown sugar in the morning. I enjoy the morning crossword puzzle and listening to Public Radio. I most of all treasure my family and friends and the memories of those no longer around.

I simply don't seem to need much to entertain myself. Yet life seems quite wonderful and profound. Life sends us on quite a frantic path to ultimately teach us the simple pleasures, don't you think?

Much love,
Sarah

Think more about the simple pleasures you've enjoyed in the past or are enjoying right now that are important to you so that you are aware every time you do them of their significance. Not major events but simple pleasures. Maybe digging in the dirt, singing in the shower, reading the paper, sipping your coffee, and watching the flies buzz in the sun. List those ordinary things that give you extraordinary pleasure.

> *To walk in a sacred manner is to make an art of life,*
> *to attend to each moment as though it were the last,*
> *to take each step as though it were the first.*
> *To breathe love and awareness into this body,*
> *entering the greater body we all share.*
> *Seeing that each step must by taken lightly,*
> *not with force.*
> —Stephen Levine, *Healing Into Life and Death*

All wise, deep things are very simple.

My business partner Frank tells of a simple encounter that illustrates how important it is to attend to and appreciate simple things. As a nurse, he was caring for a ninety-two-year-old woman with ovarian cancer who wasn't doing very well. When he brought her breakfast tray, he asked if he could open the shades and let in some sun and she said yes. She immediately said, "Isn't the sky a beautiful blue?" At first he responded with a feeble "Yeah" and continued hurrying about his tasks. When she exclaimed again about the beautiful shade of blue, he stopped and gave her his attention. She then went on to marvel at the beautiful crimson color of the cranberry juice. Since she had cataracts, Frank held the juice up to the sun for her and agreed that it was a stunning color. He then brought the flowers she had received from someone over to her bed for her to examine more closely. She sparkled and seemed so alive. The whole encounter of "being there" took only a minute and Frank wouldn't have thought any more about it, but she died that night. It struck him then that her last words to him were about the beauty in the world and, had he not paused, he would have missed what, in retrospect, was a powerful interchange.

Life becomes so elementary and simple things take on major significance for some at the end of life. Simple, but profound. Do not miss your chances to share such moments of magnificent simplicity. The sky can be so blue, the cranberry juice so crimson. A touch can mean everything. Every moment becomes a gift, an experiences in mindfulness.

> *Mindfulness is meditation in action and involves a "be here now" approach that allows life to unfold without limitation of prejudgment. It means being open to awareness of the moment as it is and to what the moment could hold. . . . [It] means being present with the food when you're eating, enjoying it rather than thinking of other things. Mindfulness means openness to the experience of motion when you walk, and to the sights, sounds, and smells around you.*
> —Joan Borysenko, *Minding the Body, Mending the Mind*

Practice for Living Each Moment

> *The solitude that really counts is the solitude of the heart; it is an inner quality or attitude that does not depend on physical isolation.*
> —Henri Nouwen, *Reaching Out*

Learn to Be Still

Take time every day to be quiet with yourself in a very focused way. If possible, make a healing place for yourself—a place where you won't be disturbed by noises from the outside, people, or telephones. Gather touchstones—comforting and empowering objects. These can be pictures of special people, places, or happenings, beautiful words or quotes meaningful to you. They might be favorite gifts, articles of clothing, or items that are symbolic in some way for you. Select mood prompters such as special books, music that delights your soul, candles, or fragrances. You can choose to ask that others not enter this special place. It can be a part of your residence or a spot in nature— your heaven on earth.

Retreating to nature is one of the easiest and most enjoyable ways to calm yourself and absorb how related you are to the earth. You smell the freshness of the air, the musty richness of the soil, the sweetness of the flowers. You observe the changes of seasons and times of more lightness, more darkness. When you are in true wilderness, you adjust your schedule to the rhythms of nature. You are not in control. You adapt. You adjust your patterns to the weather and the availability of light.

You can create rituals to revere whatever it is in nature that you find most awesome. Some like to sit or lie down on the earth, cover themselves with grass or moss or leaves, and absorb their connection to the earth. Some prefer to clutch a rock, a tight little bundle of energy that has survived for centuries, signifying permanence and exuding solidness and strength. Some like to gaze at clouds with their ever-changing personalities. Some choose to crunch across the carpet of fallen leaves in the fall.

Exercises

1. Make yourself comfortable. You may wish to lie down or sit. It is best to keep your back straight and your arms and legs uncrossed, unless sitting on the floor with your legs crossed is comfortable for you.

Relax your body. Start by tensing up your muscles as tightly as possible. Then let go and relax. Do this three times to exaggerate your awareness of how stress feels versus calmness. Then, if you choose, proceed from your toes to the top of your head through each muscle group, individually surrendering your tension.

Then shift your concentration to your breathing. Take a deep breath and focus on breathing in and breathing out. As you breathe, say to yourself simple calming phrases: Breathe in the good. Breathe out the bad. Breathe in gentle. Breathe out tension and stress. Breathe in calm for my body and mind. Breathe out smiling, feeling good.

Focus on your breathing. When thoughts appear, observe them as you would a cloud and let them float away. Return to your breathing focus. Enjoy the moment—the wonderful moment. Your mind will probably wander, but don't fret. Some days it is just harder to relax. Don't expect to be perfect. There is no way to fail. Just return to focusing on your breathing and repeating to yourself whatever calming words you have chosen. It takes practice and then more practice. Soon you will be hooked on being peaceful with yourself.

2. You don't really have to have a special place to be still and peaceful. It is best to be able to calm yourself anywhere, in a traffic jam or in a dentist chair, by concentrating on your breathing and repeating relaxing phrases. Repeat "gentle" slowly—inhale "gen," exhale "tle." Walking is a wonderful time to feel peaceful. A favorite focusing phrase while walking is to simply repeat to yourself "Still . . . ness, still . . . ness, still . . . ness" or "Peace . . . ful, peace . . . ful, peace . . . ful."

3. Find a spot in the sun, either outside or inside by a window. Stand on your tiptoes and stretch your arms as far as you can. Put your hands on your waist and twist, first to one side, then the next. Relax in a comfortable standing posture, torso erect, knees relaxed, and hands cupped in front of your hips. Focus on your breathing. Breathe in; draw the energy up from the earth toward the sky, lifting your arms, palms up, in an arc, straight in front of you. Breathe out; lower your arms to your side, bringing the energy from the heavens into your body. Repeat several times. Become the conduit between earth and sky. Feel the energy. Breathe in as you lift your arms, palms up, to the sky again. Embrace the air and the sun's rays. Know you are part of the universe. Breathe out, lowering your arms and drawing the sun's warmth to you; let it bathe your body.

4. Think differently when you are taking a walk. "Be" a part of everything you see. When something interests you, stop and absorb the beauty, think and feel your connection to the "whole." As you walk in the woods, consider how everything around you is a part of you. Imagine yourself to be a pine tree, standing firm and tall. Feel the sun, the breezes. Feel the wind through your needles, the little bird visitors on your branches. Hear their sounds.

Become the birds. Flitting from branch to branch, busying yourself with finding food, mindful of predators but enjoying life, singing your song. Or become an eagle, soaring high above—how must that feel? Watch sea gulls protecting their babies. As you walk in the woods, consider the age-old ground you are on, the history it has. Perhaps it was in the path of glaciers or witnessed beginnings of life and births and deaths and more births and deaths. Feel the harmony. As you walk, walk with beauty. See it. Feel it. Smell the earth, the pine needles, the natural decaying matter. Feel yourself in every movement. Hear each sound. Smell. Experience oneness with all life—one great unbroken life—dust to dust.

5. Close your eyes and begin to turn your attention inward. Pay attention to the physical sensations where your body is being supported by the floor or the pillow or the chair. Let yourself feel the sensation of touch and support. As you do this you may find yourself becoming more relaxed and quieter inside.

Now bring your attention to your breathing. Notice the sensation of your breath passing in and out of your nostrils as you inhale and exhale. Keep your awareness focused in that place and on those sensations. If you find your mind wandering, gently bring it back to the physical sensations. Now feel the air as it passes down behind your throat and down your windpipe. You are moving deeper inside yourself, becoming still inside.

Now feel the movement of your chest and belly, in and out, as you inhale and exhale. Settle down gently, letting go. Now feel the beating of your heart from the inside. The soft, regular rhythm of the blood moving through your body. Feel the miraculous equilibrium of your body. Concentrate on your breathing. Feel yourself centering. Now gradually begin to come back, bringing with you all the peace and calmness that you have gained, taking your own time, slowly becoming more alert, feeling refreshed.

Meaning comes in many forms. The purpose of this chapter was to help you discover and label little meanings for yourself. Once you become aware of what is meaningful and begin to seek meaning, the more you will find.

10 · Self-Care

You are guaranteed certain losses in your life. People you love die. You may lose your health. You lose some relationships, hopes, and dreams. You are not guaranteed gains. Success is learning to play whatever hand you are dealt as well as you can. One major component of that success is learning how to take good care of yourself emotionally, physically, and spiritually. In this chapter I give suggestions on how to tie up loose ends, finish unfinished business, forgive and let go. I ask you to live the Serenity Prayer, to practice accessing the wisdom deep within you. Tips on living a healthy lifestyle help you learn how to care for yourself, an art that is the backbone for any kind of renewal.

> Youth is a gift of Nature,
> but age is a work of art.
> —Garson Kanin, *It Takes a Long Time to Become Young*

Self-care involves being aware of and learning how to express your feelings. I have paid particular attention to the feelings of grief, sadness, guilt, and anger because these are the ones that most frequently block persons from moving on with life. Chapter 11 will focus on self-renewal and happier feelings.

Feel All Your Feelings

Welcome your feelings. Accept them as okay. The first step in self-awareness is to recognize what you're feeling, be able to describe the feelings, and then learn to express them appropriately. Suppressing feelings puts you out of control. Write about them or talk about them with someone, because buried feelings will fester and pop up again in some form—anger, depression, illness.

> *Young widows weep:*
> *Old widows get sick.*
> —Author Unknown

Burying your painful feelings and/or choosing to be numb takes energy. It may save pain but it diminishes the ability to feel alive. Suppressing feelings becomes a habit and the only way to break a habit is to reverse the process that formed it. Take slow, tiny steps toward being more open about your feelings. You're fighting the laws of inertia and silence. Make a move—any move. That beats just sitting there and it's a step toward being truly known and feeling more alive.

> *You can live as if life has meaning*
> *and you are a part of the web of life;*
> *or you can live as if life were chaotic*
> *and you are a victim of its whims.*
> —Joseph Fabry, *Guideposts to Meaning*

Grief expressed is grief diminished.
—Author Unknown

You don't get through life without having incredibly sad things happen to you. Then you must walk through the grieving process, not around it, to get to the light. Grief is your psychological, physiological, and sociological reaction to loss. It is normal and necessary in order to get on with life.

Once you have experienced the seriousness of your loss, you will be able to experience the wonder of being alive.
—Robert Veninga, *Gift of Hope*

You are who you are in part because of the people in your life. The closer you are to another, the more your own self and self-image are tied to them. When someone close to you dies, you lose not only that person but the part of you that is complexly intertwined with him or her. Part of you dies with the person. You then must redefine yourself without that individual.

Grief is the response to wounding. It is a process. It takes time and work to reclaim that part of yourself that goes away. And you always have a scar, you are forever changed. Not only that, but the wound can reopen—just less frequently as you heal. Certain events or memories trigger reopenings throughout life. No two people grieve the same way; there isn't a right or proper way to grieve. Additional suffering is caused by those who rigidly believe that there is a recommended order and a "proper" sequence of stages and reactions that should be followed and certain definitive feelings that must be expressed. Give yourself a break. You don't need to feel guilty because you aren't doing it right on top of the sadness and confusion you are already feeling over the loss.

How to help another. You can't assuage someone's terrible grief and pain. Let them feel it. When someone close dies, pain is the deceased's legacy to the bereaved one. No one would purposely inflict this on another, but it happens anyway when there is closeness. All you can do is let the grieving person know you are available. He or she must go through the agonizing but purifying process of grief. In *Reaching Out*, Henri Nouwen explains that "healing is the humble but also demanding task of creating and offering a friendly, empty space where strangers can reflect on their pain and suffering without fear, and find the confidence that makes them look for new ways right in the center of their confusion."

Don't expect any particular grieving reaction. What happens will happen. Some people do not show their emotions publicly. It really is okay if you don't cry at all. It doesn't mean that you are an unloving, uncaring person. It is true that most people feel better when they cry and let some of their tension out, but it doesn't mean that they are better persons than those who don't. Tears relieve pressure and serve as balm for your wounds.

Some form of confusion is usually apparent during the grieving process. More people seek professional help after a major loss because they fear they are crazy than because they are sad. They have accepted the notion that there is a right way to grieve or a certain length of time that is legitimate for them to feel terrible. They may have vivid flashes of the image of the person who has died and worry about their sanity. They may hallucinate about seeing the deceased in a crowd on television or may hear the person calling to them in the night. There is a similarity between this confusion and the searching behavior of a young child separated from a parent in a crowd. The child wanders about, not quite believing it, looking forlorn, calling out, hoping that it's not true. In the case of a death, it is true, and the denial usually occurs in strange forms, such as the dead person reappearing in dreams, opening the wounds again and inflicting more pain.

Anger usually is directed at doctors, at the person who died, at others, or at yourself. Guilt comes in the form of, "If I had only . . ." Sadness comes in many forms—gray emptiness, meaninglessness, suicidal thoughts. There is as great a spectrum of variation in the expression of grief as there are people. Some people bounce back relatively quickly. Others take a long time. There is no "appropriate" time frame. Gradually, grieving persons start to open to the world again, start learning new ways of living without the deceased. Often, with the new understanding of pain, they become more compassionate toward others. They grow in depth and fullness even though they would never have chosen that kind of learning.

Meditation for someone who is grieving (to be read by a friend). Find a comfortable spot to relax. Take some deep breaths. Notice that part of your body where you hold tension and heaviness—perhaps your head—put your thumbs on the aching spots;perhaps your neck and shoulders—massage the tender spots; perhaps your heart or your stomach—place your hands there and rub gently. Feel your feelings—perhaps a raw, searing pain of a recent loss; perhaps the accumulated personal losses of a lifetime; perhaps a pervasive, global pain about the injustices in the world. Don't analyze anything—just feel the feelings—locate the spot on your body that accumulates the pain and massage the hurt there. Breathe and feel. Breathe and feel. Press your sensitive area and massage the pain. Appreciate your pain. It is a result of caring and loving. Let the feelings come. Know that they are signs of your aliveness, your ability to care and love. Feel love for yourself. Release the pain. Feel it. Know that this is good; the only path to healing is this letting go. Breathe in the freshness, breathe out the pain. Breathe in the freshness, breathe out the pain. Appreciate your grief as the path to your own healing. Release your hands from your sensitive spot. Release the pressure. Know that this is good. Gradually return, knowing you are further along your path.

Why me? At some point philosophers, theologians, and nearly everyone else struggles with this question. You try to make sense out of the suffering you see and feel. The answer has to be arrived at individually. You all have different histories, different spiritual and ethnic backgrounds, have read different books, and will travel your own paths. You can read, discuss with others, listen and observe, but you can't impose meaning on another's experience. Grieving is an area where giving advice is to be especially avoided. How a person copes at this time is a unique process.

> *If it doesn't kill me, it makes me grow.*
> —Nietzsche

How to be with someone who is dying. At some point you will probably be with someone who is very near death. Here are some suggestion on how to "be there."

Everyone is a novice at dying and, since you only do it once, no one has any practice. As someone who cares, you are an understudy. The dying person is the main actor and directs the play. Your role is to listen, be available, and offer support—when called upon. It is the dying person's life and death.

Be there with an open heart. It is more uncomfortable for your soul to avoid being with a person than to be there. Don't say on arrival, "How are you?" Say something simple like "Hi. I've been wanting to be with you. It's so good to be here." The anticipation of discomfort is the worst part.

Don't just drop in. Call ahead and see when the best time for a visit is, and, if there's anything new about the patient's condition, you should know beforehand. Ask the primary caregiver how much time you should spend there. Give quality time. Think twice about going with several friends. It can be exhausting for the person and deprives you both of personal time together.

Let the person lead. Answer questions if asked but otherwise just be there, following his or her lead. If the person wants to avoid serious talk, fine. If he or she wants to talk or shriek about death, fine. If he or she wants to cry, fine.

Determine, if you can, what the person does want. Present openings. (Do you want to talk? Do you want to listen to music?) Don't push.

Ask what you can do and do it. Make phone calls, read a story, answer correspondence, shop.

If the person can't talk, assume he or she can hear and act accordingly. Don't exclude the person from conversations with others.

If the person expresses anger and says seemingly irrational and hurtful things to you, depersonalize the statements. Frustrations are sometimes overwhelming at this time. Back off.

Say what you need to say. Don't allow your discomfort or the awkwardness you feel prevent you from taking the precious moments to let the person know how important he or she is to you, what particular impact he or she has had on you, so that this person you care deeply about will know that he or she has made a difference, thus becoming immortalized

Bring pictures for reminiscing.

Don't give advice or rattle on about your philosophy of life. This is an important, rich time for the dying person, who has personal answers and a personal journey to take.

Speak clearly but don't shout. A common error for visitors is to assume that a sick person can't hear.

Don't patronize or talk baby talk. Use a respectful tone.

Don't give false assurances. "You'll get over this. It won't get you. Don't worry, everything will be all right." Give believable assurances. "I'm going to be here with you. We'll do everything we can to make you comfortable."

Resist offering solutions and beliefs. If the person vents great fury at dying, at being robbed, and is full of "why me's?" or "why do I need to suffer like this?" or "I want to die," the listener is often tempted to launch into expounding on solutions and beliefs. Resist this. Just listen. It is not up to you to have an answer. " I don't know" is fine. Answers need to come from the patient. Don't give advice or try to sell your beliefs. This is not your journey.

Don't take the person's defenses away. The person has a personal history, personal experiences, and personal defenses. Trust the person, in most cases, to control his or her own denial.

Don't say "cheer up" or "count your blessings." Don't rob a person of the right to feel bad or sad and don't be hard on yourself if nothing seems to help.

There are many things that you can do:

- Offer to pray with or for the person.
- Provide opportunities for the person to express feelings.
- Treat the person as still living—not dying.
- Give information the person requests.
- Offer a back rub or a massage.
- Help the person tie up loose ends if he or she wishes.

Specific suggestions for words to use:

- "I'm here."
- "Do you want to talk? About anything in particular?"
- "Do you have pain? Is there anything that I can do to help?"
- "What music would you like to hear?"
- "Is there any favorite book, scripture, poetry, or letter that I could read to you?"
- "How can I make this room as perfect as possible for you?"
- "This is a mysterious time."
- "This is hard work for you; you're doing a good job."
- "Do you have any advice for me?"
- If the person wants to reminisce, say, "Remember the time . . . What was the best period in your life? What are you proudest of?"

Guilt is pervasive. A little guilt is balancing but the great majority of it is worthless. People feel guilty for doing too much, for doing too little, for what they have or haven't said or done, and for what they even think about saying or doing. Balancing guilty feelings is very difficult for some people. As Erma Bombeck says, "Guilt is the gift that keeps on giving."

Societal. Society has its own guilt-producing norms. For instance, it is almost impossible for a family not to feel guilty about placing a parent in a nursing home, even when it is the best possible solution. A more recent "new age" phenomenon is to feel guilty or bad if you are sick, getting old, or dying. Advertisers and the media inundate the public with messages that say if you eat right, exercise, and think right, you won't get old, sick, or die. This is obviously untrue, and it only wastes valuable energy to feel guilty on top of feeling sick. The odds of your dying are quite impressive—one out of one.

You definitely can improve your chances of having a better, more enjoyable life by taking care of yourself and working on your attitudes. You need to be aware of the subliminal toll that advertisements take by such slogans as "defeat aging" or "get rid of ugly baldness" in order to seduce you into buying anti-aging pills and creams, camouflaging your gray hair, and making you feel guilty about perfectly normal events. It is a sad testimony that old persons often are horrified by the face they see in the mirror. Societal standards have made aging difficult.

Church-related. Another source of guilt is the church. "No ills befall the righteous and the wicked are filled with trouble" (Prov. 12:21). People believe they are being punished when bad things befall them. A little of this kind of guilt can keep some people on the straight and narrow, but once again, carried to the extreme, this simply doesn't fit the facts. The painful death of a child, a plane crash, an earthquake just randomly happen in this imperfect world.

Another favorite guilt-producer is, "This is a test. God only tests those who can bear it." You need to keep in mind three factors: nature is morally blind; people have choices and some choose evil; death is natural.

Family-induced. Some family systems are accomplished at heaping on guilt. The following example is a typical guilt-producing statement followed by a good nondefensive response. Mother: "Elsie's daughter comes every day to visit her." Daughter: "I know you would like to have me come more often. I wish I could. I come when I can."

Self-induced. "I should have called mother." "I should . . ." Your own "shoulds" are perhaps your largest source of guilt. Some level of this self-induced guilt is good and legitimate, but too much makes you unreasonably hard on yourself and even dysfunctional. Ultimately you are your own worst critic. The ability to forgive yourself is a skill that can be learned.

Worry does not empty tomorrow's sorrow;
it empties today of its strength.
—Corrie ten Boom, *A Gift of Hope*

Anger

Anger is an emotion that people often can't express well. It has many aliases and degrees of intensity. It is often described in other terms, such as frustration, apathy, hurt, sorrow, or disappointment. Early in your life, many of you probably got the message that "it's not nice to be angry." This is nonsense. Feelings are not right or wrong; they just are. You have them and it is important for you to recognize and express them. A trait of a mature person is the ability to express anger in a mature way. It is best to bubble anger out as you become aware of it instead of suppressing it completely or storing the energy until it erupts in an inappropriately excessive way. The energy cycle of anger is as follows:

1. Because of unmet expectations, abuse, loss of respect for yourself or another, you become aware of your feelings of anger. You feel anxious, disappointed, uncomfortable, or powerless.

2. You feel an energy buildup.

3. Relief occurs only after expression of this energy.

"Unexpressed anger." There is no such thing as unexpressed anger. It goes somewhere. If not expressed appropriately, it reappears as one of the following:

Depression. Learning to express anger constructively is much better than becoming depressed, which usually flattens people, making them withdrawn and nonfunctional. Anger often gives you energy. It is not a "bad feeling." It probably has produced more good in society than love, the epitome of "good feeling," because anger is often action oriented. Anger toward injustice has brought about more change in the world than love of justice.

Physical symptoms. When release of anger is inhibited, it manifests in tension headaches, stiff necks, high blood pressure, inability to have satisfying sex, low back pain, and the onset of many diseases. Dr. Dean Ornish has researched anger and hostility and found that you can reverse cholesterol buildup in your arteries by improving your eating habits and using stress reduction techniques to reduce your anger.

An explosion. The anger has festered to such a degree that the smallest incident can cause a reaction disproportional to the triggering event. Explosions scare people away and inhibit the possibility of constructive communication.

Passive-aggressive behavior. Anger leaks out in indirect and often unconscious ways. Passive-aggressiveness can take the form of cutting sarcasm, inappropriate humor, or hostile statements. Since the anger is expressed indirectly, it is often hard to pick out. The recipients just know that they have been hit and that it hurts. Another common example of passive-aggressiveness is when you receive a compliment that has a hook in it, such as: "You look so nice; I didn't recognize you"; "Congratulations—I'm surprised you've done so well . . . must have been in the right place at the right time"; "Can't you take a joke?" (the punch in the arm after a snide remark); "It's so nice of you to visit me for a change."

Let your anger bubble out.

Appropriately expressing anger. You don't want to suppress your anger, nor do you want to let it accumulate until there is an explosion. It is best to bubble it out as you become aware of the feeling. If you are beyond the bubbling stage, a particularly satisfying technique for releasing anger is to engage in physical activity such as brisk walking, racquetball, jogging, dancing, aerobic exercising, or chopping wood. Other safe, satisfying, and appropriate releases of built-up anger are screaming loudly in your car when you are alone or lying on your bed kicking, flailing, and wailing, or beating on a pillow. A quieter means of expressing anger is a good assertive response. (The following section explains how to act assertively.) Anger is an internal directive. It is important to recognize it and claim it, as you do when your body has a temperature and you know something is wrong. When you're angry, you are being given a message. Here are the steps for expressing anger:

1. Recognize the feeling. This takes practice. Mentally healthy people can have as much anger as the emotionally ill. The trick is how anger is expressed.

2. Identify the source of the anger. The intention is not to "get back" at another. Find a willing third party or professional upon whom to vent the energy.

3. Verbalize your anger in a healthy way:

- Describe what is bothering you. Be specific, such as "You don't look at me when I talk to you."
- Express what you are feeling, using the "I" message. "I feel insignificant and all alone when you do that."
- Ask explicitly for a different, specific behavior, such as, "If you'd just look at me when I'm talking."
- Emphasize how a change would make it better. "I think that the atmosphere around here would improve for you, too." This is an example of a good assertive response.

Other people's anger.

Practice active listening versus reacting in kind. "You sound sad and hurt. You sound really miffed about this. That really means a lot to you."

Use time out. "We aren't getting anywhere. I'm going to leave now and come back when I feel more able to deal with this."

Ignore or have broken record response (repeat the same response over and over). "I hear you . . . I hear you . . . I hear you . . ."

Unfinished Business

What do you have to do for yourself to have peace of mind?

If you could change one decision that you've made, what would it be?

Are there things that happened to you that you haven't forgiven or you just can't forgive?

Are there things you did that you haven't forgiven yourself for?

Your answers to the above questions are your unfinished business, which is very individual. Some folks feel okay about loose ends; other need to tie matters up. Completing unfinished business is your business and only your business. It is not about making other people accept you. It is not about approving or forgetting. It is not about expecting anything in return from anyone else. It is between you and you. It is one of the paths toward peace of mind.

The end of unfinished business is forgiving yourself or another, the means whereby you can experience peace. By no longer judging, you release the past and your fear of the future. Forgiving means that you have learned and are no longer oppressed. Until you forgive someone, you are in competition with that person and you are losing. You are captive and cannot move forward.

It is important to know that you cannot rush forgiveness. You don't want to trivialize your feelings by saying things such as "they did as well as they could" until you have gone through the justifiable anger. Only then is it possible to determine that it is not worth your energy to hang on to the hard feelings any longer. Some acts are unforgivable and it would be a self-violation and more abuse to yourself to forgive them. Forgiving does not mean that you are a sin pardoner. You do not have any authority as a human being to forgive from a position of superiority. Often the action or cruelty itself can't be forgiven but the person can be forgiven for having temporarily lost his or her humanity.

Often the person hardest to forgive is yourself. Humans are enormously hard on themselves, usually much more merciless on themselves than they ever would be on others. People hold on to their self-hate and recrimination for decades. Had they been sent to jail for their perceived crimes, they would have been out years ago. Learn how to forgive yourself. Take pride in your ability to survive, your resourcefulness, and your stamina.

There is no way to get through life without making mistakes on occasion. Being hard on yourself saps energy and gets you absolutely nowhere. It is self-abuse. Being cruel to anyone is wrong and that includes cruelty to yourself. Self-forgiveness breaks the pattern of self-abuse. You can decide to let up on yourself and feel the weight of the world drop off your shoulders.

Forgiveness means to let go. Since there's barely enough time for loving in this world, there's certainly not enough time for hating. Remember, forgiveness is not about the other party. It is about you. It is about taking charge, no longer allowing the abuser to hold the trump card. You cannot save him or her but you can save yourself. You may carry with you rage, unmet expectations, fear, blame, resentment, and denial. Because of this, it is easy to block out the possibility of light and love and precious growth. Not forgiving is like punishing someone by holding your breath; you are the one who is turning blue. It's a vicious cycle. By insisting on being the victim, you become your own abuser. Ask yourself, "Who am I hurting?" If you are wasting a lot of energy hating someone, are you not really handing over another victory to that person? Say to yourself, "For my own integrity and survival, I choose to no longer give away any of my energy. I choose to be the boss of my own self. I can decide to let go of this and no longer be captive."

Finish the unfinished business that looms in your mind. Unresolved business interferes with resolution of subsequent life tasks. Don't put off saying what you have to say or doing what you have to do. Even if the person is dead, you can write a letter dealing as fully as you can with the issue. Whether or not to write or contact a person who is living depends on the situation.

The ability to let go allows you to finish unfinished business. Sometimes there are specific activities you can do or feel the need to do. Other times, opening your heart, releasing the toxins of the past, releasing whatever has prevented you from connecting with another is enough. In those instances, completing unfinished business can be accomplished simply by changing your outlook. Your friends and family may sense this change as evidenced by the numbers of times individuals or families have delightedly reported to me, "He has changed, you know."

This ability to be different in your relationships often happens at the end of life because you have nothing to lose or you simply haven't the energy to be any other way. It is bittersweet that so many conversions happen at the very end of life. Fractured communication and old hurts build up in families, separating them like steel barriers. Then, even when there is a strong, foundational love, it is hard to penetrate the wall.

Sometimes the path through this wall is a specific act of forgiveness. Often it is letting go of the past, clearing the fog, and showing a new ability to live in the present. Sometimes a general statement, such as, "I am a new person. Starting today, I am changed," announces this transformation. Other times change happens and is gradually observed. The mark of a person with no unfinished business is one who appreciates each moment and lives life so fully that "doing" takes a backseat to simply "being."

Completing Unfinished Business

With yourself.

- Write your feelings down in detail.
- Ritualize them. Let them go bit by bit. Put them on paper and burn them in a campfire or fireplace. Say, "It is finished!"
- Feel a load drop off your shoulders—savor the lightness and freedom.

With someone else.

- Use the "I" message. "I feel terrible that I wasn't around more when you were in your teens. I would do it differently if given another chance. I missed out and messed up. I am sorry." This is for you, not for the other. Speak of your feelings. Acknowledge what you feel bad about. Don't blame. Don't accuse.
- Make your message direct and clear.
- State what you want but don't force it.
- Have no expectations of others. You are doing this for yourself. You can't count on the other person's reaction. At the very least, you can know that you attempted it and won't have to live with "I wish that I would have . . ."

With someone who has died or is gone. You need not be with the person. It is your work on yourself that is important. It does not take two people to release the tension and antagonism that blocks completion. This means opening your heart, feeling the pain, and releasing it and all the encapsulated energy it holds. Only when you decide that pride and resentment are no longer worth the toll they take are you able to move on.

To concretize your change of being, you may choose to ritualize this process. Some persons set the stage by arranging a special place, gathering significant memorabilia and appropriate music to create an ambiance conducive to a major event. Some go to a favorite place in nature, stretch out in a meadow, sit beside a stream, or go outside on a starry night and begin an imaginary dialogue with the particular being with whom there is unfinished business.

Meditation for Letting Go or Forgiveness
This can be directed to Jesus, God, your Higher Power, to the air, or to the universe.

To another
"I, (your name), ask (their name) for forgiveness for . . . Please free me."

To self
"I forgive myself for my past unknowings and deeds, those that were intentional or unintentional. I want to love and care for myself and let go of the weight I carry. May this be the first moment of a new and free me."

Of another
"I, (say your name), let go of the pain and hurt that I have felt in this relationship. It prevents me from living my life fully in the present. I no longer want to waste my energy or allow these feelings to have any power over me. I want to be free."

Unfinished Business: Suggested Action Chart

Unfinished Business	Action Taken
Past regrets, unexpressed words or feelings	Even if the person is deceased, write a letter or say out loud to yourself or another what you want to say. If regret is about an event or decision, let go of it.
Present/future un-expressed words or feelings	Write or tell the person what you need to say. If you have unspoken hostilities or great anger, work through it with a professional. Plan what to do next.
Self-care	Let people know what you want.
	Rework your diet.
	Schedule exercise.
	Plan quiet time.
	Plan pleasurable activities that make you feel good.

Planning

Informal:

State your wishes

Study the options

Formal:

Formulate a will

Health-care declaration

Financial planning

Unfinished Business: My Action Chart

Unfinished Business	Action Taken
Past	
Present/Future	
Self-care (be specific)	
Planning	

Live the Serenity Prayer

> *O God, give us*
> *serenity to accept what cannot be changed,*
> *courage to change what should be changed,*
> *and wisdom to distiguish the one from the other.*
> —Reinhold Niebuhr.

There is much freedom in changing what can be changed. There is also great freedom in changing your attitude about things that you cannot change. You cannot change what other people do. You cannot change your genetics, the weather, natural disasters, floods, tornadoes, your predisposition to disease and virus. You can only change yourself, your own thoughts and actions. Whenever a problem or dilemma arises, ask yourself these questions:

1. "Is this something that can be changed?"

2. If yes, "Is this something someone else can change but is out of my hands?" It helps to name to yourself whose problem it is.

3. "Is this something I can do something about?"

Run Any Problem Through This Process

Problem	Can't change	Someone else can change	I can change

Learn to Be Still and Center Yourself

Centering is a process that helps you pay attention to your being, not just your doing. It helps you step away and look at yourself and what you are doing with some compassion and clarity. It is a physiological as well as psychological and spiritual process. Techniques include breathing exercises, prayer, meditation, yoga, Tai Chi, affirmations, and much more. Some people use centering phrases such as, "One moment at a time," "Be gentle with yourself," "God (Jesus, Holy Spirit), be with me."

It is important to learn how to step back and calm yourself. Find a way that works for you and helps you attain a new perspective. You may find that reading, gardening, walking, swimming, or taking a bath works for you. Centering time is precious; set aside time for it daily. Some of you may choose to commune with your God or Higher Power or with that wise old person deep inside you who knows you well. Or you may simply choose to visualize a person who loves you very much standing beside you. This presence knows what you have been and what you are yet to become. Imagine that this presence is filled with great love for you and is there to help you channel your energy in a positive way. If you commune with this presence, you can find help with your questions and choices.

Visualize the most beautiful sky you have seen, the most staggering sunset. Feel it. Breathe in deeply. Try journaling, writing down your thoughts. This helps many people center. Singing and chanting repetitive words in a rhythmic manner is a way of centering and has been practiced in many cultures since ancient times. This allows you to express beauty and connectedness. Musical instruments, especially drums, help you reach a primal place inside of you. The first sound humans hear is the rhythmic beat of their mother's heart. Celebrate! Speak from your heart.

Maintain a Healthy Life-Style

Maintaining a healthy life-style is fundamental to self-care. Your health habits greatly affect how you age. If you have had poor eating and exercising habits, you begin to feel the consequences in older age. Physical fitness doesn't necessarily lengthen your life, but it improves the quality of life because you feel better. It is never too late to start a good program. The focus of this book is more on the emotional and spiritual realms of your being, but the importance of how you take care of your self physically cannot be separated from the rest. The tendency is not to notice or appreciate the wondrous fluidity and balance of your body until something doesn't work quite right. When something is out of kilter, whether physical, mental, or spiritual, your attention is caught.

This chapter has focused on ideas for taking care of yourself. What do you need to do to improve in the areas of:

- Feeling your feelings?
- Finishing unfinished business?
- Living the Serenity Prayer?
- Centering yourself?
- Maintaining a healthy life-style?

11 · Attitude

Your attitude is your most priceless possession. With all the mysterious unknowns and losses in your life, the one thing you can control is your attitude. You can decide to make the best out of any situation you face.

What we believe is the most important option of all.
—Norman Cousins, *Human Options: An Autobiographical Notebook*

Attitude is a dynamic, perceptual process. It is never static. Making an effort to remain positive in your attitudes gives you an upper hand. Bad things happen and you need to work through the pain of the grieving process, letting the sad or mad feelings surface before you can get on with living life fully. If you don't develop the capacity to look at the bright side and refuse to dwell on misfortune, you simply make life more difficult for yourself. Your attitude can neutralize the negative impact of losses.

> *It is just as easy to help yourself to a bit of heaven*
> *as to a chunk of hell,*
> *and a good deal more intelligent.*
> —Jerome Ellison, *Life's Second Half: The Pleasure of Aging*

It takes a conscious effort for most people to be positive. The most practical and simplest way to look at a difficult situation is to simply ask yourself, "What is my choice?" Ultimately, when bad things happen, your choices are to be miserable and stay miserable or to make the best of it. Many cope because they are forced to. This isn't about idealistic, new attitude formation. You cope or you don't. It is as simple as that. Often, your attitude is what people remember most about you. Attitude seems to transcend other physical and personality traits. A person with a positive outlook on life is the one who has a gleam in the eye, an aura, a sparkle that shines through. On the other hand, you know people who seem to walk under a gloomy cloud, whose worst fears often seem to happen. Similarly, the lighthearted, positive people appear to make good things happen. This is no accident and it isn't magic. You can cause good things to happen to yourself. When you have this positive outlook, you get the added bonus of a presence so desirable to others that you are invited to share their special experiences with them.

Brendon O'Regan reports that, in addition to the plain common sense of it all, research has finally substantiated what has long been suspected. Your mental and spiritual outlook directly affects your physical health. C. B. Pert, A Goodheart, and E. Rossi report about respective studies that show that a negative attitude undermines your immune system. This will be discussed in more detail later, but the facts indicate that you simply can't afford to be depressed. Depression makes your body sick. What to do or say to yourself to remain positive varies from person to person. For example, this rationale worked for John: John figured out that his hatred of George was making him dysfunctional and preoccupied. Not only that, it was really a victory for George. When competitive people realize that they are using up valuable energy resenting, hating, or being victimized by their obsession with another, and that the only way they are going to emerge victorious is to let go, matters are simplified. One day in the office, John, after years of simmering, said resolutely, "I'm not going to let myself go under. I'm going to start letting go of these destructive feelings and concentrate on making the most out of my time. I'm beginning to see that, if I succeed at this, I will have truly won." And he proceeded to do so.

S. Kobasa's and M. Puccetti's 1983 research showed that people with a combination of three attitudes were least likely to become ill:

1. Persons who view tasks they face as challenges or opportunities.

2. Persons who feel they have choices and a great degree of control over their own fate.

3. Persons who feel that they have a purpose for living.

They said that people with these three attitudes exhibit "hardiness." They found that this quality of hardiness was "three times more powerful as social support and exercise put together in determining who gets sick in times of stress."

You can manipulate your brain. When you nurture it with positive, hopeful thoughts, your mind eventually comes to believe what you are telling it. There is truth to, "Fake it until you make it." Your brain is not necessarily your friend. It cannot be trusted. It hears whatever it is told and your body reacts accordingly. You can befriend it by intentionally feeding it believable thoughts that lean to the positive. Feelings are honest. They are barometers of what you are thinking. It is your thoughts that can be controlled. You can choose your thoughts, attitudes, and outlook, and thus your way of being.

Be yourself. Purposefully decide to like the person in the mirror. That is you. Do for yourself whatever makes you feel healthy and good. There can be no denying that you will feel better when you take care of yourself physically as well as mentally. This may mean working on your posture, your diet, your dental care, or an exercise program. There is a predetermined path to feeling good about yourself. For some it includes dyeing the hair, getting rid of the gray; a face lift, getting rid of the wrinkles; having a tummy tuck, getting rid of the sag. Whatever makes you feel good about yourself is okay. But you need to be careful and aware that there's a delicate line between doing what you do to feel good about yourself and denying your true self, attempting to feel superior to that person in the mirror. There comes a time when you can no longer stretch middle age. Just be aware of what you are doing. The most freeing path seems to be to welcome aging and avoid getting caught in the all-American fight to check the advance of every wrinkle and deny your own aging self. There are certain attitudes and traits that make for successful living no matter what your age.

> *The person who learns to play the guitar at 80
> will be playing at the resurrection.*
> —John Bratner

Traits for Successful Living at Any Age

Ability to see holiness in everyday things
Ability to lighten up—be optimistic
Willingness to be vulnerable
Compassionate intelligence
Ability to express feelings
Ability to give and receive
Genuine interest in others
Awareness of feelings
Good listening skills
Willingness to risk
Celebrative spirit
Lifelong learning
Clear boundaries
Sense of purpose
Sense of wonder
Sense of humor
Playfulness
Enthusiasm
Sensitivity
Flexibility
Resilience
Curiosity
Courage
Hope
Joy

> *Live in perpetual astonishment.*
> —Theodore Roethke

Positive Self-Talk

It is hard not to feel good if you have these traits and attitudes. A basic psychological premise is that you "feel according to how you think." So it follows that, if you want to feel better, you need to learn to put more positive thoughts into your head. The media makes it difficult by subtly and not so subtly filling you with negative thoughts about aging. Learn to counteract any catastrophic statements you hear or find yourself muttering with less extreme statements. If you want to look forward to a satisfying old age, stop emphasizing the negative and blaming everything that goes wrong on aging. For example, so often you hear people say, "I'm feeling old" whenever they feel sick. When you are sick, you are sick, not old. You need to practice converting your negative self-talk to positive. Here are some examples:

Harmful Self-talk	Positive Self-talk
"Retirement scares me silly. My whole identity was tied into my job. Now what will I do!"	"It's so exciting to think of all the things I can do now. It's like starting a new life!"
When people grow old they become more fault-finding, rigid, and irritable.	When *some* people ___ , *others* soften, loosen up and seem to relax and enjoy life more.
"I didn't sleep very well. I have a headache. This is going to be an awful day."	"I'll take it easy. It'll feel good to have a relaxed day. I'll take a walk; that always feels good."
"Oh no! My face is getting so wrinkly. I can't stand to look at myself."	"Another wrinkle—another battle scar. Sure is better than the alternative."
"I feel so tired and run down and I have some new aches in my leg. It must be another of those things that happens to you when you get old.	"I feel ___. I'm going to make an appointment with the doctor to see what's wrong."
"I can't find my keys. This is it—I've definitely got Alzheimer's."	"I can't ___. What a pain! I periodically pull stunts like this."
"Nobody gives a hoot that I'm so lonesome. People really don't care."	"I'm having one of those days. I'd better call somebody over for coffee. I always feel better if I do something."

"I'm so stupid. I can't even understand these insurance forms."

"These forms are really complicated. I'll go get help."

"My daughter hasn't called all week. I'm such a burden. I must have done something wrong."

"I haven't heard from Mary. She is really busy. I sure miss her. I wonder if she is free for lunch."

"What a mess I am. I look like an "old bag."

Well, I'll never win a prize, but I like this old body. It has served me well."

"I'm over-the-hill. It is downhill from here."

"I'm over-the-hill and I'm picking up speed."

Affirm Yourself

Healing is about getting to know and like yourself. There are several ways to work on this. While it's important that you insert affirmations into your mind, they must be believable. If the statements you choose are impossible, such as, "I am tall, slim, and athletic," when none of it is true or possible, don't bother saying it. Affirmations must have some semblance of possibility for your mind to take them seriously.

You can waste enormous amounts of energy when you're hard on yourself. You are your own worst critic and your negative self-talk can do some deep damage. Each thought directs your path and is responsible for how you are feeling. You can change your feelings by ridding yourself of negative beliefs and replacing them with affirmative thoughts. Suggestions are:

- I can make this a great day.
- I have choices.
- I am changing and that is good.
- I can ask for what I want.
- I can choose where to direct my energy.
- I can make someone else feel good today.
- I will get through this.
- I am a strong, capable, caring person.
- I am having a fulfilling and fun old age.

Before you get out of bed in the morning, get in the habit of focusing on something positive and good in your life. Identify one activity that gives you pleasure to pursue that day. Then get out of bed and start your day with an upbeat attitude and a plan for the day. Make a list of your own personal, helpful, and hopeful self-talk. Put your list in an accessible place to grab when you are feeling unsure of yourself.

Self-Affirming Thoughts

It's easy to forget what you do well when you're feeling down. These may be simple or complex tasks such as cook, manage the checkbook, tell stories, or relational tasks such as "I am/was a good friend to . . ." or "I communicate well with . . ."

This is what I do well.

"Others appreciate me because . . ." (Ask others.)

"When I've had difficult times before in my life, I've coped by . . ."

> *It is funny how you can stand more than you thought*
> *and feel yourself inside get stronger,*
> *and taste the salt of your own wounds*
> *and the weight of things that have happened to you.*
> —Meridel LeSeuer, *Ripenings: Selected Work 1927-1980*

Reframing

One person walks through a woods and sees nothing. The next person can walk through the same woods and have a peak experience.

> *Old age, to the unlearned, is winter;*
> *to the learned, it is harvest time.*
> —Author Unknown

Nossrat Peseschkian in *In Search of Meaning* relates the story of an Asian king who had an anxiety-provoking dream. He dreamed that all his teeth fell out, one by one. Disturbed, he called in his dream interpreter. The dream interpreter listened sorrowfully to his dream and disclosed to the king, "I have bad news for you. You will lose all your relatives one by one, just like teeth." The interpretation aroused the anger of the king. He had the dream interpreter thrown into a dungeon. Then he had another dream interpreter come. This one listened to the dream and said, "I am happy to make a joyful interpretation. You will live to be older than all your relatives, you will outlive them all." The king was overjoyed and rewarded him richly. The courtiers were amazed at this. "You actually didn't say anything different from your predecessor. But why was he punished and you rewarded?" The dream interpreter answered, "We both interpreted the dream the same way. But it depends not only on what one says, but also on how one says it."

You give yourself power when you learn to reframe your thoughts in a more positive way. It is an on-going job to neutralize the negative messages received from society in general and sometimes from persons such as doctors and clergy, who are in positions of authority. For example, the informed consent documents that you are asked to sign prior to an operation are frightening to many. If you read the chemotherapy protocol that often accompanies the diagnosis of cancer, you will probably find only intimidating, technically vivid descriptions of all that could go wrong. It is important to be given information but it takes courage to sign up for procedures after you've read a list of possible side effects and have not been given one balancing word of encouragement or hope that you might be healed or comforted.

It is important for you to reframe what getting old means to you. Keep in mind that what "aging well" means to one will be different to another. It is a value-laden concept. How one chooses to age depends totally on your values and beliefs. There are multiple pathways for your journey.

Old Age

> No Spring, nor Summer
> beauty has such grace
> As I have seen in one
> Autumnal face.
> —John Donne

"Old" means what you want it to mean. Many things that are old are considered beautiful—antiques, canyons, stumps, and rocks and gems. Think of what being weathered and wrinkled symbolizes. Think of the additional perspective given to you by having lived a great number of years. Old is relative. Malcolm Cowley tells of Supreme Court Justice Oliver Wendell Holmes, who, when he was ninety-four, spotted a pretty girl and lamented "Oh, to be eighty again!"

Late life is a period of complex richness. You can see it as a time of great transition and opportunity, a time to remove the filters and masks you may have put in place when you were younger, a time to heal wounds, a time to reap the benefits that you've worked so hard for, and, finally, a time to enjoy hard-earned pleasures. If you have been dreading old age and thinking of it as a time of loss and regression, you can reframe this belief. Late life can be anything.

Getting older has a lot of positives. You can finally discard frenzied living and linger with beauty in ways that the "fast track" didn't allow. Older age can be a time of great authenticity, with less need to please others or to put things off. A great illustration is the story of the ninety-four-year-old who announces she's going to get a divorce after seventy-two years of marriage. "Why?" she was asked. "I've been waiting until all the kids are dead," she replied. Discarding the pressure of pleasing others often becomes possible for the first time in old age. You are finally your own boss. In old age, you are closer to tapping into your unconscious mind and, after a lifetime of rich experiences, you are better able to appreciate your similarity and connectedness to others.

> *You can't have true splendid fullness*
> *until you're at least seventy years of age.*
> —John Bratner

> *Successful old age often amounts*
> *to playing a poor hand well.*

Reframing is the process of using more life-enhancing and hopeful words and concepts. For instance, births and beginnings are described positively as blooming, new, wondrous, and hopeful. On the other hand, death and endings often bring to mind descriptors such as failure, unwanted, and terrifying. Endings are as integral a part of living as beginnings. Beginnings and endings are part of the ongoing cycle. Endings are beginnings. They are marker points indicating the phase of life and growth that you are in. Examples of reframing are:

Examples	Destructive	Reframed
wheelchair, cane, walker	symbol of deterioration of body	helpful tools, enabling mobility and maintenance of independence
person with illness	victim	resilient survivor
independence	"I won't accept any help."	"If I accept some help I will be able to be independent longer."

The real voyage of discovery consists not in seeking new landscapes, but in having new eyes.
—Marcel Proust

Independence

For most older people, maintaining independence is a priority. The majority choose to live close to their families and dread the time when they might have to lean on their children or others for any sort of help. Our society stresses the importance of independence, which, although a natural and necessary developmental stage, is overplayed to such an extreme that it makes the normal changes and often increasing dependency of old age seem mortifying and degrading. Instead of feeling comfortable with asking for help when one's physical capabilities diminish, many elders feel distressed and saddened and their self-esteem plummets.

This pattern will continue until society reframes its thinking about the interaction between doing and being. As long as you continue to define your success and self-worth in terms of what you do, instead of viewing success as your way of being, your way of relating to the world and to each other, it's going to be hard for the very old to feel worthwhile. As long as it is independence that is idolized, instead of seeing interdependence as the umbrella under which independence and dependence play alternating roles, it will be difficult for the frail elderly to feel good about themselves.

Courage

Who are the most courageous of all? Many of the frail elderly exhibit more courage on a daily basis than any other population. Their deeds certainly don't get the headlines that the younger, healthy, adventurous sorts who challenge mountains and white water do. Their deeds may appear humble, but if the measure includes degree of difficulty, they are major victories. Many frail elderly persons model how to face limitations and increasing dependence on others with a grace and dignity that needs to be appreciated.

It takes courage for the chronically ill to keep plugging along knowing there is no cure for what ails them, that this is no temporary trial but a long trip downhill, an inevitable physical decline. It takes courage for the painfully arthritic just to get out of bed in the morning when they seriously doubt if their wobbly legs will hold them up. It takes courage for the dignified elderly to venture out to eat when they fear spilling and embarrassing themselves and others. It takes courage to continue crocheting afghans with your shaky hands when you know that the finished product won't be what it used to be. It takes courage to simply look in the mirror and see an old face and say, "Hey, I like the way I look, wrinkles and all," when society seems to be saying, "Be ashamed of those wrinkles; keep looking young," as if there is something unnatural or wrong about aging. It takes courage to be responsible and give up your driver's license and all that freedom when you know your eyesight and reactions are no longer good enough. It takes courage to find the balance between letting people know how you feel and what you need, while being able to get out of the narrow world of aches and pains and be genuinely interested in the feelings and activities of others. It takes courage for caregivers of the chronically ill to "stick with it" when their energy is being drained, and, despite all their efforts, their loved one is getting worse. It takes courage to swallow your pride and ask for help. You all know people who exhibit this kind of courage. This is a kind of courage-by-default that most of you hope you'll never have to know. You like to think you will live a healthy, relatively carefree, full life and then die suddenly and painlessly in your favorite chair. A few do. And, factually, you are living longer, healthier lives. This improvement and the technological triumphs that increase longevity have only postponed having to look at the calloused attitude toward those who are no longer as able and have less control.

It takes courage to wake up and learn from this age group. They are the ones with more experience. They're facing their limitations. They know death is the end of life, and they force younger people to look at the illusory nature of always thinking that there is a "cure" for whatever ails you. They know that their bodies won't get better or younger.

Older people are quietly waiting for society to respect one's full life cycle, to stop worshiping the young, the unblemished bodies, and to recognize that it's the spirit, what's inside that body, how one thinks, feels, and acts that is most significant. Older people exhibit a reverence for life and heightened sensibilities to the beauty of otherwise ordinary events. They have a wholeness and perspective about what is important that you rarely find in younger people.

*It is time to learn from these frail teachers,
let them know what you are learning, and that
you appreciate their courage.*
—Trish Herbert, *Who Are the Most Courageous of All?*

Self-Esteem

Your self-esteem is a valuation or a judgment you make about yourself. It isn't static. It is an ever-changing process. It's based on messages from the past. That's why it is so important to review your past to see what those messages are so you can claim and perpetuate the positive and discard the negative ones. You can intervene and convert your negative judgments of yourself so they need not become self-fulfilling, a presumption of what you'll be in the future.

Your self-esteem fluctuates throughout your life. It is one of the mysteries. You are what you believe, but your beliefs are not necessarily true. You can rework and challenge your negative beliefs. The criteria for raising one's self-esteem are:

- Getting to know yourself.
- Recognizing and owning your feelings.
- Recognizing and focusing on your strengths and competence.
- Taking responsibility for planning what you can.
- Educating yourself to existing options.

This book is a road map for raising self-esteem. If you participate and practice its many suggestions, you will be well on your way.

Assertiveness

Another important and closely related skill is communicating assertively. What does it mean to be assertive? Assertiveness is in the middle of the spectrum of response between nonassertiveness (passivity) and aggressiveness. Learning to be assertive is a critical component of self-care. People who are able to assert themselves feel confident and capable. The following table helps describe the differences among assertive, aggressive, and passive people.

Passive	Assertive	Aggressive
avoids conflict	communicates directly and honestly	controls, dominates
recognizes the rights of others	recognizes own rights and rights of others	recognizes own rights
lacks confidence	confident	hostile, cocky, may or may not be confident
allows others to choose for them	chooses for self	chooses for others
builds up resentment and anger	deals with anger	acts out anger in attack mode
little self-respect	respected by self and others	generates feelings of hostility
hard to get to know	promotes authentic relationships	no one wants to get to know you
voice soft and wimpy	voice well modulated and firm	voice strident and loud

In addition to being passive, assertive, or aggressive, two other response categories are often used. Some of us are *socially compliant*. It is one step up from being nonassertive because a decision is made to not respond assertively. It is a choice. *Passive-aggressiveness* is an indirect, dishonest, double-meaning response—often expressed through humor. Recipients of this behavior find this much more difficult to handle than pure, blatant aggressiveness.

Test Your Assertiveness

Response Categories: 1) Passive; 2) Socially Compliant; 3) Assertive; 4) Passive-Aggressive; 5) Aggressive

There is one example of each of the above categories for each scenario.
Identify each category and circle the response closest to your own.

1. You question the treatment the doctor is suggesting. You

   a. say nothing, do what doctor says.

   b. challenge doctor's competence—demand an explanation.

   c. ask doctor for more information: give your opinion; request feedback; if not satisfied, seek a second opinion.

   d. go along because the doctor has been right before.

   e. ask doctor how much money is in it for him or her.

2. The person you visit is lonely. She wants you to spend Sunday afternoons with her. This is inconvenient, but you are aware that she views "No" as a personal rejection. You

   a. feel there is no choice; come on Sundays.

   b. explain that Sunday is inconvenient—refusing in an understanding manner.

   c. say, "Forget it, maybe I shouldn't come at all."

   d. say you'll come—plan to have someone call up and cancel.

   e. try to come some Sundays.

3. You've made reservations at a restaurant with two friends. At the last minute, another friend arrives and asks to come along. You don't want to include her. You

   a. invite her along.

   b. tell her that you have been planning to be with your other friends that night and would prefer making plans with her for another time.

c. say, "Lots of nerve. You should have called first."

d. allow her to come, but ignore her all evening.

e. invite her along so you won't hurt her feelings.

4. Your partner, friend, or spouse continually interrupts and appears not to be listening to what you are saying. You feel angry. You

a. say, "It hurts and makes me mad when you interrupt all the time. You've been doing it a lot lately. Please be aware of it and stop."

b. do nothing.

c. say, "You would learn more if you would listen more."

d. excuse him or her because this behavior is not usual.

e. jokingly say that it must be difficult to carry the full burden of the conversation.

5. You are waiting in line to get into a popular movie. This line is one hundred feet long and as you get up to about five feet from the ticket booth, menacing motorcycle riders butt in line right in front of you to grab the last tickets. You

a. back off.

b. tell them in a loud voice to get to the back of the line.

c. choose to be quiet to protect your physical health.

d. ask them politely to go to the back of the line.

e. kiddingly say, " I wish I were a macho stud."

6. You are chairperson of a committee at church that has to complete a project in a week. All of your committee members, except one woman, have worked hard. You

a. divide up this woman's work unobtrusively among the other committee members.

b. confront the person and dismiss her from the committee.

c. do most of the woman's work yourself.

d. tell the person that she is not doing her fair share and request that she do so.

e. complain to others on the committee about her behavior.

7. You have been thinking about completing a living will. You say to yourself,

a. "It's time for someone else to get saddled with some heavy decisions for a change."

b. "Why bother? The doctors will do what they want anyway."

c. "I don't want to think about it."

d. "Time to take some responsibility. I am going to do it."

e. "I'd do it but I just don't think that anyone would want to talk about this stuff with me."

Response category rating of each question:

1. a—1, b—5, c—3, d—2, e—4   Response Categories
2. a—1, b—3, c—5, d—4, e—2   1. Passive
3. a—1, b—3, c—5, d—4, e—2   2. Socially Compliant
4. a—3, b—1, c—5, d—2, e—4   3. Assertive
5. a—1, b—5, c—2, d—3, e—4   4. Passive-Aggressive
6. a—2, b—5, c—1, d—3, e—4   5. Aggressive
7. a—5, b—4, c—1, d—3, e—2

Are you assertive? The intent of the above exercise is to aid you in understanding what is meant by being assertive and to demonstrate that, even though assertiveness is the preferred response ordinarily, the dynamics of the situation (as in question #5) affect your response.

Boundary Setting

Setting limits with others is a form of assertiveness. Learning to say "no" to requests or demands that go against your own internal needs is a symbol of self-respect and self-caring. Congratulate yourself. Claiming your boundaries and setting limits is always a delicate proposition and easiest to do early versus later in a relationship. This is a way to teach people how you wish to be treated. If you continue to accommodate others and don't make boundaries for yourself, you soon lose the respect of others. For example: "I don't like the way you're talking to me"; "I feel unjustly attacked, frustrated, and sad"; "I'm going to hang up the phone now. I'll call back tomorrow and see if we can communicate better." Learn to initiate rather than react. For example: "This is what I'd like to do . . ."; "I've decided to organize my life a little more. Could you please limit your calling to between 8:00 and 9:00 A.M. or 5:00 and 6:00 P.M.? That would be a big help"; "I need some time to talk" (to a support group).

Thriving or Surviving?

Robert Butler and Myrna Lewis describe good mental health in old age as the ability to thrive rather than just survive. You spend a certain percentage of your life doing important survival tasks, some pleasurable, others not. In order to live fully, you need to plan time for truly thriving. Estimate how you spend your time and rearrange the tasks in the appropriate thriving or surviving category (e.g., perhaps preparing meals is a joy for you and belongs in the thriving category). Monitor yourself for a week. Total up the number of hours and divide by seven days to determine average time spent thriving or surviving.

Time Log

	M	T	W	Th	F	Sa	S	Total	Average
Survival Tasks									
Eating, preparing meals									
Personal care									
Sleeping									
Shopping, errands									
Housework, chores									
Waiting for something									
Working									
Other _____									
Thriving									
Reading									
Meditating, praying, centering									
Working for pleasure									
Volunteering									
Loving, being a friend									
Participating in games, sports									
Traveling, planning									
Hobbies									
Other _____									

Can you increase the number of hours dedicated to thriving?

Pleasurable Activities

List activities that give you the most pleasure. Make a plan for increasing their frequency. When you are aware that you enjoy doing something, however mundane it may seem, get in the habit of saying to yourself or, even better, say out loud, "I like this. This is really living!"

Mind/Body/Spirit Connection

Your attitude affects your physical health. Reflect on the fact that you are a complex being. You have a physical body, a mind, and a spirit making up the whole you. You have been living in an age that has overemphasized the physical, scientific explanation of disease. Common sense tells you that disease and illness are often associated with stress and emotional imbalance, that they are directly related. And this has been supported by scientific research, gaining acceptance even among cynics. It has been demonstrated that stress and depression undermine the efficiency of the immune system.

Every cell in your body communicates by way of psychoneuroimmune chemicals to other cells. That is why your heart races when you think of something that excites you. It is why you blush when embarrassed. It is why, when I was caregiving for my mother, I lost my taste and smell for ten months, then regained them the day after she died. It is why you feel better when you smile. It is known that laughter sparks your healing endorphins. There is literal power in the art of thinking healthy thoughts. S. M. Simonton reports that "denial has been shown to exacerbate an existing disease. In one of the early psychological studies of cancer, Bruno Klopfer was able to predict which patients would have fast versus slowly growing tumors by measuring the amount of denial the person used. Those with a strong need to maintain an image of 'looking good' when they were in emotional pain had the fastest growing tumors."

Suppress your feelings and your stomach keeps score.

Of course your emotional state is just one of the factors in contracting or recovering from an illness. Your genetic make-up, life-style, diet, and the environment in which you live are just a few of the other factors involved in complex interactions. The tendency to repress feelings is a common characteristic of cancer patients, yet, when whole communities have been exposed to radioactivity or deadly bacteria, some people have lived, while others died. Several factors are involved. Consider the following experiments illustrating mind/body/spirit connection:

1. The subjects for this research had traditionally had positive skin reactions to tuberculosis testing. A positive reaction means one has had or has been exposed to tuberculosis, and once the reaction is positive, it stays that way. The subjects were trained to expect a positive reaction in their right arms and to expect no reaction to the saline (salt water) injected in the left arm as a control. Then, unknown to them, the saline and the tuberculosis test substances were switched. Their bodies continued to react according to their expectations, not the actuality. L. Dossey reports the results: "Their reactions to the tuberculosis skin test material, which they now believed to be saline, were reduced from an area of redness and hardness with a mean of 15 millimeters diameter to one of only 4 millimeters. Their expectations seemed capable of overriding the purely automatic physical responses of the body. Their bodies had clearly begun to behave according to the dictates of their thoughts and not according to mindless internal processes. "

Phase two of this experiment had a subject intentionally and knowingly modify her reaction to a tuberculin skin test through visualization, which she was able to do. What interested the scientists most was that when her immune cells were removed from her body and studied in test tubes, she had not only affected her skin test response but the actual cells themselves.

2. Dr. David Spiegel, professor of psychiatry and behavioral science, conducted studies on the effects of psychosocial support for very ill women with metastatic breast cancer. It is noteworthy that Spiegel was not a believer and set out to disprove that intervention such as support groups and hypnotherapy would improve quality or length of life in these women. He worked with eighty-six women, dividing them into an intervention group and a control group.

In the support groups a great deal of caring developed among participants. They learned to use their cancer to prioritize their needs and wants and help their friends and family, giving life and the experience of cancer some genuine meaning. The study's initial results were that the sensation of pain caused by metastatic cancer increased in the control group and decreased in the group with psychosocial support. Pain rating was twice as high for the control as for the intervention group. This study was published by David Spiegel et al. in the early 1980s. There are similar studies, such as those by M. Cohen and L. LaFave et al., illustrating that changing one's focus and attitude helps one handle the disease better.

3. Other studies have indicated that women who come for biopsies that show malignancies have an inability to express anger (e.g., S. Greer and T. Morris, D. A. Goldstein and M. H. Antoni). On the other hand, being too angry and too expressive is also harmful to your health. It is that middle area—appropriate expression of anger—that appears to be most life enhancing.

Studies substantiate clinically what intuitive, thinking beings knew all along. You feel better having someone care; kids somehow feel better when their parents kiss their "owies"; you sometimes get sick after a lot of stress; and you may even have some control over your dying, as repeatedly evidenced by people holding off death until a grandchild is born, a birthday is celebrated, and so on.

Leonard Inskip reports studies that indicate job dissatisfaction can damage workers' health and may explain why heart attacks peak between 8:00 and 9:00 A.M. on Mondays. He quotes Larry Dossey as saying, "The best predictor of longevity is not physical exams, family history, or sophisticated tests, but how people feel about their health. . . . Researchers went to a Pennsylvania town where people live long lives. They expected joggers and health nuts. They found people overweight and smoking. But the town was like one extended family; that affects attitudes and emotions. . . . We human beings may not be capable of understanding how something as ethereal as an idea can influence something physical, but people should try."

4. The world of the brain is an overwhelmingly wondrous machine that is just beginning to be understood. In *Head First*, Norman Cousins describes it this way: "A computer has not been devised that can match the potential capacity of a human brain." The brain dispatches millions of little messages throughout our body. Dr. C. D. Clemente describes how this transmission of information works and how emotion is physically produced. She discusses the difference in the body between the touch of a hand of a nonemotionally bonded colleague and the touch of a lover's hand. A gesture like this sets off many electrochemical reactions from tiny neurons originating from the five senses and the organs. Mind/body interaction is complex, but the spirit

is also an important component of your whole being and perhaps the least understood. The distinction between your physical, emotional, and spiritual parts is simply not clear.

5. Prayer has been researched and found to be a powerful force in healing. L. Dossey reports that Dr. Randolph Byrd of the University of California assigned 393 patients admitted to a coronary care unit of San Francisco General Hospital into one of two groups: 1) a group that was prayed for by home prayer groups around the country or 2) to a group not remembered in prayer, using random, double blind rigorous scientific measures (neither the patients or the nurses and doctors knew group assignments). Byrd defines prayer as "connecting with a higher power." People in the prayed-for group had five to seven persons praying for each of them. The findings found that the prayed-for group were five times less likely to require antibiotics, were three times less likely to develop pulmonary edema, and did not in any case require mechanical ventilating support while twelve in the unremembered group did. The implications are far-reaching.

Scientific studies are proving over and over that how you think affects the progress of disease. To recognize this is to be empowered. It means you can affect your health. There are many new kinds of interventions gaining popularity. Some physicians are ordering alternative therapies such as guided imagery, stress-reduction programs, biofeedback, and primary care physicians instead of specialists. J. Rattenburg reports that in 1967 there were nineteen medical doctors for every osteopath; today the ratio is nine to one. There are more chiropractors and osteopaths because they are more willing to look at the whole person. There is a delicate line between accepting a diagnosis and getting all the treatment available and either total denial at the one extreme or being fatalistic about your prognosis at the other. The goal is to "aim for the middle"—squeeze into that area of belief that does not deny, accepts a "maybe," but helps to develop determination to live every moment and make the most of the situation.

At a deep level, your mind, body, and spirit are not separate. Your whole aging process can be reshaped by what you think. Every thought brings a corresponding chemical reaction. Negative thoughts convert into tensions that impact your body in harmful ways. You must program your body toward health. Use the positive self-talk and affirmations discussed earlier. It all adds up to this: when you're told to "work on your attitude," the suggestion isn't benign sweetness; it is critical to your health and well-being.

My Spiritual Legacy

Whenever you think to yourself or find yourself saying some brilliant, meaningful words, write them down. A venerated Jewish custom of bequeathing a spiritual legacy to others includes leaving messages or words to live by through an ethical will. Here are some suggested introductory sentences:

- I write this to you, (their name), in order to . . .
- These were the formative events of my life . . .
- These are the people who most influenced me . . .
- These are some of my favorite possessions that I want you to have and these are the stories that explain what makes these things so precious to me . . .
- Some of the scriptural passages that have meant the most to me . . .
- These are the mistakes I most regret having made in my life that I hope you will not repeat . . .
- I would like to ask your forgiveness for . . . and I forgive you for . . .
- I want you to know how much I love you and how grateful I am to you for . . .
- These are some of the important lessons that I have learned in my life . . .
- These are some of the memories of you I cherish . . .
- The best advice I ever got was . . .
- These are some messages that I would like to leave my (friend, partner, spouse, child, grandchild, niece, nephew) . . .

What words do you want to leave?

Ethical Will

Universal Lessons of Late Life

Most older persons are very pleased with life. Though they have been pressured to fear old age, study after study reports that they are pleasantly surprised when they actually get to that stage of their lives.

> *"This is the best time of my life. I love being old."*
> *Why is it good to be old? "Because I am more myself*
> *than I ever have been." "I am happier, more balanced . . .*
> *and better able to use my powers."*
> —May Sarton, *At Seventy*

Some of the hard-learned lessons of late life are:

1. *To age well means taking responsibility.* Successful aging doesn't just happen. You have decisions to make and actions to take to increase your chances of being able to thoroughly enjoy this rich period of your life. You may have to make attitude adjustments.

Each day is a gift.

2. *Aging teaches you to make do with what you have.* Your body has a built-in obsolescence to it, but unlike "things," you cannot replace the parts that wear out (with the exception of some modern transplantation). Making do, adjusting, and maintaining are the keys to successful physiological aging. You have witnessed that people wealthy with "things" are not necessarily happy. It appears it is not quantity that makes for happiness but rather it is the quality of what you have. Many older adults have learned the lesson of "enough is enough." You don't need a great abundance of things. You

need enough money, security, health, meaningful activities, closeness with other people, basic comforts, faith and hope. Older people choose, or are forced, to get off the fast track of middle-age and learn the value of simplifying their lives.

3. *It is harder to receive than to give.* You may recognize that relationships involve interdependency, but it is the independent part of interdependence that is the most comfortable. Accepting limitations and becoming more dependent on others is difficult. Remaining as independent as possible yet asking for what you need is the fine line that older persons must negotiate. Modeling this delicate balancing act—doing the best you can and then asking for help when you are no longer able to do it yourself—is a tremendous gift you can give to those you love.

4. *Accumulated experience acquired over the years gives one an overview unavailable when younger.* Getting older doesn't guarantee wisdom or spirituality but it does provide the foundation of experience to support them. Late life can be a time for reflection, pulling together loose threads and weaving them into meaning. Late life allows you to view life as a whole, to see the patterns and ways you have changed. You can see life's erratic nature and learn that the deaths and losses were as necessary as the joys and rebirths. Hard times force change, open the heart, and are often turning points that cause you to do some major reprioritization and reconnection with others. You know by now that you are vulnerable. Bad things happen to you, not just to the people down the street. In *The Measure of My Days*, Florida Scott-Maxwell reflects on her life in her eighties, saying:

> *In silent, hot rebellion we cry silently—"I have lived my life haven't I? What more is expected of me?" Have we got to pretend out of noblesse oblige that age is nothing, in order to encourage the others? This we do with a certain haughtiness, realizing now that we have reached the place beyond resignation, a place I had no idea existed until I had arrived here.*

> *It is a place of fierce energy. Perhaps passion would be a better word than energy, for the sad fact is this vivid life cannot be used. If I try to transpose it into action I am soon spent. It has to be accepted as passionate life, perhaps the life I never lived, never guessed I had it in me to live. It feels other and more than that. It feels like the far side of precept and aim. It is just life, the natural intensity of life, and when old we have it for our reward and undoing. . . . Some of it must go beyond good*

and bad, for at times—though this comes rarely, unexpectedly—it is a swelling clarity as though all was resolved. . . . It may be a degree of consciousness which lies outside activity, and which when young we are too busy to experience.

5. *Societal standards do not make getting old easy.* Society constructs barriers that are hard to hurdle. Values such as the need to be productive make some older people feel that they have outlived their usefulness. The media and advertisers make it hard to feel good about how you look when the continual emphasis is on avoiding wrinkles, baldness, white hair, and so on. Older people, like any oppressed group, are asked to accept societal standards and assimilate. Just as nonwhites are pressured to "look" white, gay and lesbians are more accepted if they look straight, young women are asked to adopt male rules in the business world, old people are driven to look young and adopt standards of middle age to be more acceptable.

6. *Older persons become more at ease with their own mortality.* You accept the reality that the time you have left is forever shortening. Some people learn to live one day at a time earlier in life, but in late life, most recognize their finiteness and the necessity of living every moment knowing that it might truly be their last. Studies repeatedly show that there is an inverse relationship between age and fear of death. Young people fear death far more than older people.

7. *Life is a balancing act.* A recurring theme in taking caring of yourself and developing a beneficial attitude is learning the fine art of staying in balance. Late life can be a time of gloom or a time of promise and fulfillment. Finding the balancing point between the following conflicts of late life is a major developmental task of older adults: controlling and planning/letting go; accepting and adjusting to losses/pushing yourself to do more; needing to "do" to feel good/just "being"; achieving comfortable dependency/independent way of living; facing mortality/living fully. This is a delicate business. You each will find your own line depending on your particular set of circumstances. "Everything in moderation" seems to be a key for successful living at any age.

8. *Late life can be a period of great satisfaction and contentment.* It can be a time when the spirit thrives. It can be a time of continued learning and growth, the hallmarks of health at

any age. There is increasing acknowledgment that the goal of finding meaning and making sense of your life is as least as awesome a project as any challenges or gifts that come with your earlier years. Late life is a time to reap the rich rewards of a life well lived and grow stronger from within. Nothing is more hopeful than witnessing older people who have experienced the ups and downs that life brings and are still hopeful, energized, and embrace life.

Hope is an orientation of the spirit and the heart;
it is not the conviction that something will turn out well,
but the certainty that something makes sense,
regardless of how it turns out.
    —Vaclav Havel

Self-Renewal Checklist

Gather items that give you comfort and pleasant feelings—pictures, favorite gifts, books, music, stones, other meaningful objects. Create a special place where you can escape to be with yourself and feel peaceful. This book suggests several ways to center yourself: My Humor Journal (p. 40), Peak Moments Chart (p. 129), Self-Affirming Thoughts (p. 165), Ethical Will (p. 182).

Conclusion

The Vintage Journey provides a framework for you to collect the many pieces of your life, giving you a sense of why and how you have lived and affirming your "whole being"—your humanity. Affirming your journey as a totality is the spiritual task of aging. By talking about yourself, your values and experiences, you have described your very essence, your soul. Your own story is your best teacher. For instance, when you answered the question "Tell me about someone who has been important in your life, and why?" you named what you value. Talking about past experiences attributes meaning to them that you may have been unaware of at the time and, in fact, can interpret more accurately now than when they were happening. When you are in the middle of a muddle, you view the experience subjectively and from a narrow context. It takes time and distance to see clearly.

Clarity is power. On your odyssey toward wholeness, I hope that you have become aware of both your uniqueness and your similarity to others. You've been given the opportunity to plan responsibly for your future, tie up loose ends, recall choice wonderful moments, and appreciate your many strengths. You may have seen that the interruptions, the surprises, and the detours on your journey have given you some of life's richest experiences. You have many choices and there are rich opportunities in this later stage of life, different from those of younger people, but just as exciting and potentially fulfilling. Hopefully the insights you have acquired through this reflective journey will give you the tools and the wisdom to live the rest of your life as fully as possible. Follow your wisdom. Enjoy!

Appendix A

Guidelines for Taping Your Story

The oral tradition, handing down family wisdom, humor, and history, has been carried on since the beginning of humankind. Let's not forget the importance of another's story.

Variations

1. *Self*-record your own story. Give it as a gift, your legacy

2. Interview *another*. This can be either totally other-oriented—you only ask questions and listen—or it can be an interaction between two or more participants.

3. Record the hubbub, laughter of a *group/family* occasion.

Rules

1. Ask for permission if taping another.

2. Set a special time/sequence of times.

3. Give the storyteller some lead time so he or she can look over this book and decide what areas are of interest. If you are the initiator, have your questions ready.

4. Bring along props to trigger memories (photos, old newspaper headlines, articles, etc).

5. Check and recheck your tape recorder or video camera. Use power cord over a battery-powered recorder, if possible. Do you need an extension cord? Use sixty-minute tapes (thirty minutes per side); longer tapes are more likely to distort voices or become damaged.

6. Find a quiet, suitable place for recording with as little outside interference as possible. Take the phone off the hook.

7. Introduce the tape. Tell the date, place, occasion, the name(s) of those speaking. Write the same information on the cassette.

8. Set a time limit and be aware of the storyteller's energy level. Make an appointment for the next interview time, if desired.

Appendix B

The Art of Listening

If you are playing the role of a listener, nothing is more fascinating than understanding another. This is a person waiting to be discovered. You have an opportunity to learn. It is not altruistic listening. Ideally, you are not listening for their sake, but for your own. You are reliving another's life, empathizing with their feelings, creating a respectful atmosphere where it is safe for them to be honest. It's a time to "be there"—not to judge, advise, or analyze. Acknowledge how important this is to you and reciprocate by sharing your own views or stories if your partner prefers that. Let your partner set the tone. Travel with the storyteller—let him or her take you along on the journey. Your listening is a gift of time.

Be gentle. Don't push. Let your partner pick and choose what he or she wants to reflect upon. If you are the initiator of this exploration:

> Explain why you want to do this.
>
> Ask for permission. If granted, set a time.
>
> Pick a place that minimizes interruptions.
>
> Be aware that interviewing can be tiring and stop before exhaustion. Agree on a future time and place.

There is an art to listening well. It is an act of love. It is an action, not passive. You are demonstrating by your listening that you care; that simple action is far more powerful than words.

Pay Attention

Concentrate on the person. Let go of all other thoughts for now. You are not here to deal with your fears or problems. Maintain eye contact. Speak distinctly. Get rid of any avoidable outside distractions such as television, radio, visitors. Be respectful.

Let Speaker Know You Are Listening

Encourage the speaker to keep talking. Check out what you think you are hearing by periodically repeating what you hear, using the speaker's words or your own. Observe nonverbal cues and comment on them when appropriate.

Ask for Clarification

If it's not clear to you what the speaker is saying, don't assume anything or let it pass. Check it out. Say, "Am I hearing you correctly?"

Don't assume that your solution to a problem is the speaker's solution.

Be Empathetic

Aim to understand the speaker's point of view. This means "getting in his or her shoes" and looking at the world from that perspective. Listen for meaning and feeling. Encourage description of feelings.

Be Supportive

Communicate your concern and caring in an atmosphere of warmth and acceptance. Keep aside any judgmentalism that you may feel. Most of the time being supportive will be very natural, but, even if you are unable to agree with the speaker's point of view, you can always be supportive with comments such as "this has been hard for you" or "it's good that you're talking about these things." Look for parallels of agreement. Support does not mean "I'll solve your problems for you" or that you necessarily agree with the speaker.

Limit Your Own Talking

Keep the focus on the speaker and off yourself and your opinions. This is his or her time. Your role is to ask appropriate questions in order to help you both become more aware of the speaker's values, feelings, or wants. An exception to this occurs if you have agreed that this is to be an exchange of stories instead of a one-way exploration.

Don't Give Advice

The objective of active listening is to help the speaker figure out how he or she feels or what he or she wants to do. You are a facilitator in this process. You may point out options or express your opinions if requested. It is not your responsibility to tell the speaker what to do, to fix the speaker, or to make him or her happy. The speaker may distort stories. Listening without fixing or correcting can be very difficult. But if you truly listen, he or she will probably come closer to the truth.

Be Respectful

You are modeling respect for yourself, for others, and the storyteller. Be prompt, reliable, and able to set limits. Tell the speaker how much time you have to spend and when you can do it again.

Encourage Recognition and Expression of Feelings

Focusing on feelings is a core ingredient to effective active listening. A goal is to create an atmosphere of acceptance of feelings—any feelings—without judgment. Bringing feelings into awareness is the first step in a process of change or acceptance. Don't invalidate the speaker's feelings by false cheerfulness. Tell the speaker what you are learning. Help the speaker find proof of his or her own competence.

Don't Demand "Truth"

Remember this is the speaker's story—not yours. This isn't the time to demand truth. A story is a person's interpretation of an event, who was there, what and why events occurred. In *Crossing Open Ground*, Barry Lopez describes his thoughts about dignity and truth: "I think of the dignity that is ours when we cease to demand the truth and realize that the best we can have of those substantial truths that guide our lives is metaphorical—a story. . . . Truth reveals itself most fully not in dogma, but in the paradox, worry and contradictions that distinguish compelling narratives—beyond this there are only failures of imagination. . . . We are more accustomed now to thinking of 'the truth' as something that can be explicitly stated, rather than as something that can be evoked in a metaphorical way. [Truth] is something alive and unpronounceable. A story creates an atmosphere in which it becomes discernible as a pattern." Storytelling isn't a science. When you listen to another's story you are viewing the experiences as the speaker sees it. Listening is caring, not judging or correcting.

Empower Them

The deepest act of love is to help persons love themselves. Your purpose is to help them help themselves. By active listening you are saying:

- I am interested in you as a person and respect your thoughts.
- I know that they are valid for you.
- I am not here to change or evaluate you.
- You are worth my time.
- You can trust me.
- I think what you feel is important.

By asking good questions you can help others access their strengths. Look for signals of what makes the person feel adequate. The interactive quality of questions such as, "How do you feel?" "What do you think about your diagnosis?" "How do you perceive treatment?" delivered in the spirit of "let me be part of your life" or "let me understand" or even "let's figure this out," if there's a problem, helps the cared-for person feel loved, empowered, and has the potential for renewing the person's faith in his or her own abilities.

Appendix C

Legal and Ethical Terms

Note: States have slightly varying definitions of some of these terms. Check with authorities in your state for accuracy.

Advance directives. Legal documents in which competent individuals can retain some control over their health-care decisions in the event they are no longer able to do so for themselves. A living will and durable power of attorney for health care are the most common examples. Living wills in several states have a section in which you can designate a proxy with authority to make decisions on your behalf when you are no longer able.

Assisted suicide. Occurs when a patient kills himself or herself after having been given information and/or assisted by another in gaining access to the means for committing suicide.

Best interest standard. When a person is no longer able to make a judgement for himself or herself and has not let his or her wishes be known, a surrogate decision-maker determines what would be in the person's best interests according to societal standards.

Competent (in medical context). A person able to make decisions for himself or herself. Legally, a patient is considered competent to make a decision if he or she has the ability to understand relevant information about the medical problem and the consequences of the decisions about treatment.

Conservatorship. When a person is determined to be unable to make his or her own decisions and has not previously designated a person to make decisions, a court can appoint a conservator or a guardian to handle financial and personal decisions. You may plan for this situation by predesignating a conservator in a written document and giving instructions regarding how you would want your personal and financial matters handled.

Durable power of attorney for health care. A legal document that appoints another person to make health-related decisions for you in case you are unable to do so. This extends the authority of the power of attorney beyond death, thus making it "durable." This legal device is an important alternative to guardianship and conservatorship and allows the designated attorney-in-fact to make health-care decisions for the principal when he or she becomes incompetent or unable to make his or her own decisions.

Euthanasia. The active killing of a suffering patient.

Guardianship. The most extreme form of surrogate decision-making. If a person is declared incompetent to make his or her own decisions, a guardian can be appointed by the court to make all decisions, including health care. A person under guardianship permanently loses his or her right to vote.

Incompetent. A person is determined to no longer be able to make his or her own decisions.

Life-prolonging measures. Treatment that is likely to prolong the natural process of dying when there is no significant hope of functional recovery. Examples could include resuscitation or artificially administered nutrition.

Living will. A written statement, which is a legal document in many states, in which a person who is still able to make competent decisions can state his or her wishes and instructions about the kind of medical treatment he or she would want if terminally ill and unable to directly provide that information. A proxy decision-maker can also be named in many state living will forms.

Power of attorney. A legal device that permits one person known as the "principal" to give to another, called the "attorney-in-fact," the authority to handle his or her banking and real estate affairs. This authority lasts as long as the principal is competent and capable of delegating that authority.

Proxy. A person legally named to make decisions for another.

Substituted judgment. Making treatment decisions that the patient had verbalized to you while competent.

Surrogate decision-maker. An individual approved to make judgements or decisions for another. There are several types: designated proxy, designated attorney-in-fact in durable power of attorney for health care document, guardian, conservator, and decision-makers using either the "best interest" or the" substituted judgement" standard.

Terminal illness. A terminal condition is an incurable or irreversible condition for which the administration of medical treatment will only prolong the dying process. This broad definition would apply to many types of incapacitating conditions, such as being permanently unconscious.

Will. A legal document that designates what happens to one's property and assets when one dies (does not involve health-care decisions).

Appendix D

Health-Care Terms

Artificial feeding and hydration (food and fluids). In situations where a person is unable to take in food or fluids by mouth or swallow or eat in a manner adequate to sustain life, a tube may be inserted into a vein (hyperalimentation), through the nose (nasogastric), or directly into the stomach (gastrostomy) for purposes of providing liquid nutrition and hydration on an ongoing basis.

Cardiopulmonary resuscitation (CPR). In the event that the heart, blood pressure, and breathing fail to the extent that death is expected within minutes or seconds, rescue measures are taken such as pounding on the chest, inserting a breathing tube into the windpipe, and administering medications and electrical shocks.

Chemotherapy. Drugs used in the attempt to treat and control disease. The chemicals frequently have some side effects.

Coma. Comatose patients are in a sleeplike state and are unarousable due to damage to the brain stem. Comatose patients do not usually experience the long-term survival of persons in a persistent vegetative state.

Do not hospitalize (DNH). When nursing home residents for whom the experience of hospitalization would be more confusing and painful than the therapeutic gain would warrant, DNH orders are established by prior agreement of the resident and his or her surrogate decision-maker.

Do not intubate (DNI). An order declaring that the patient should not be given artificial nutrition or hydration through tubes.

Do not resuscitate (DNR). A request that resuscitation (CPR) measures not be initiated because the patient and family in consultation with a physician have requested such an order on the patient's chart. A statement about resuscitation is frequently required for patients with a terminal condition in which resuscitation may serve only to prolong the dying process. Such an order can be reversed at any time and should be reviewed at regular intervals to determine if the DNR order should remain.

Do not treat (DNT). When placed on a patient's chart, the decision has been made to limit treatment to what is available and not to initiate life-prolonging treatment. Factors that are considered include assessment of physical or emotional pain, prognosis, and the risks and distress caused by the proposed interventions. Comfort (palliative) care is the focus.

"Higher brain" concept of death. The irreversible loss of the capacity for consciousness and social interaction, thus focusing on the cognitive aspects of being human versus the traditional loss of ability to function organically. Death occurs when those functions that are irreplaceable—cognitive functions—are lost. The criteria are the irreversible loss of the neocortical brain and cerebral functions that are responsible for cognition and consciousness.

Hospice care. A philosophy of caring for terminally ill people that provides symptom and pain relief and emotional and spiritual support for the patient and his or her family and friends. It is a physician-directed, nurse-coordinated team approach that may take place in the home, hospice center, nursing home, or hospital. Care is individually designed to deal with dying, death, and grief in the last phases of a terminal illness.

Irreversible chronic illness. Usually a long-term illness that worsens over time and is not reversible. Treatment is usually for the symptoms instead of the cause, as the cause is usually not known. Persons may be capable mentally and/or physically. Examples include Alzheimer's disease and rheumatoid arthritis.

Kidney dialysis. A process used to remove unwanted fluid and waste products from the body when the kidneys are unable to do so. The blood is purified by being pumped from a patient's artery through a kidney machine and returned to the body through the patient's vein.

Life-prolonging measures. Treatment that is likely only to prolong the natural process of dying when there is no significant hope of functional recovery. Examples could include resuscitation or artificially administered nutrition.

Limited time trial. The use of medical measures for a specified period of time to determine whether the benefits will outweigh the burdens.

Palliative care. Symptom and pain relief without prolongation of life, emphasizing comfort and improved quality of life.

Persistent vegetative state (PVS). When a person's higher brain is dead but the brain stem still functions. Since the brain stem regulates vegetative functions such as respiration, swallowing, and regulation of sleep cycles, a person in this state is awake but unaware. The person always requires artificial food and nutrition but often does not require a respirator for breathing. A person can live for a long time in this state (thirty-seven years is the record).

Respirator/ventilator. Mechanical breathing machine that assists a patient's breathing when he or she is partially or totally unable to do so on his or her own. The patient is connected to the machine with a tube directly through the windpipe or through the nose to the windpipe. This process provides volumes of air and adequate oxygen to support life.

Slippery slope argument. The domino theory applied to health care. The fear is that if you allow one action that is acceptable, you begin a downhill slide leading to similar actions that are unacceptable.

Terminal condition. An incurable or irreversible condition that without the administration of life-sustaining treatment will, in the opinion of the attending physician, result in death in a relatively short time, which typically means six months or less.

"Whole brain" theory of death. A person is considered brain dead only when the entire brain—including the brain stem—is dead.

Appendix E

Sample Legal Documents and Responses

(Consult your attorney or the state legal services developer about the laws in your state.)

Living Will Declaration

To my family, relatives, friends, physicians, clergy, and all others whom it may concern:
Declaration made this _____ day of _____, 19 _____ (month, year).
I, _____ (full name), being of sound mind, willfully and voluntarily make known my desires that my life shall not be artificially prolonged under the circumstances set forth below, do declare:

1) If at any time I should have an incurable injury, disease, illness, or condition certified to be terminal by two physicians who have personally examined me, one of whom is my attending physician, and the physicians have determined that my death is imminent, whether or not life-sustaining procedures are utilized and where the application of life-sustaining procedures would serve only to artificially prolong the dying process; or alternatively, if I have been diagnosed as being in a persistent vegetative state, I direct that all artificial life-sustaining procedures be withheld or withdrawn and that I be permitted to die naturally with only the administration of nutrition, medication, or the performance of any medical procedure deemed necessary to provide me with comfort care or to alleviate pain.

2) In the absence of my ability to give further directions regarding my treatment, including life-sustaining procedures, it is my intention that this declaration be honored by my family and physicians as the final expression of my legal right to refuse or accept medical and surgical treatment, and I accept the consequences of such refusal.

3) I understand the full importance of this declaration and am emotionally and mentally competent to make this declaration. No participant in the making of this declaration or in its being carried into effect, whether it be a physician, spouse, relative, or any other person shall be held responsible in any way, legally, professionally, or socially, for complying with my directions.

_____
Declarant's signature

The declarant is personally known to me and is, to my judgment, of sound mind.
I am at least 18 years of age and

- not related to declarant by blood, marriage, or adoption
- not the declarant's attending physician or employee of the attending physician, or a patient or employee of the medical care facility in which declarant is a patient
- not entitled to any portion of the declarant's estate on declarant's death
- have no claim against any portion of the declarant's estate on declarant's death

Witness _____
Address _____
Witness _____
Address _____

County of _____
State of _____

Subscribed, sworn to and acknowledged before me by _____, the declarant, and subscribed and sworn to before me by _____ and _____, witnesses, this _____ day of ____, 19 _____.
My commission expires:

_____

Notary Public

[Seal]

Minnesota Health-Care Declaration

Notice:

This is an important legal document. Before signing this document, you should know these important facts:

(a)   This document gives your health care providers or your designated proxy the power and guidance to make health care decisions according to your wishes when you are in a terminal condition and cannot do so. This document may include what kind of treatment you want or do not want and under what circumstances you want these decisions to be made. You may state where you want or do not want to receive any treatment.

(b)   If you name a proxy in this document and that person agrees to serve as your proxy, that person has a duty to act consistently with your wishes. If the proxy does not know your wishes, the proxy has the duty to act in your best interests. If you do not name a proxy, your health care providers have a duty to act consistently with your instructions or tell you that they are unwilling to do so.

(c)   This document will remain valid and in effect until and unless you amend or revoke it. Review this document periodically to make sure it continues to reflect your preferences. You may amend or revoke the declaration at any time by notifying your health care providers.

(d)   Your named proxy has the same right as you have to examine your medical records and to consent to their disclosure for purposes related to your health care or insurance unless you limit this right in this document.

(e)   If there is anything in this document that you do not understand, you should ask for professional help to have it explained to you.

TO MY FAMILY, DOCTORS, AND ALL THOSE CONCERNED WITH MY CARE:

I, _____, being an adult of sound mind, wilfully and voluntarily make this statement as a directive to be followed if I am in a terminal condition and become unable to participate in decisions regarding my health care. I understand that my health care providers are legally bound to act consistently with my wishes, within the limits of reasonable medical practice and other applicable law. I also understand that I have the right to make medical and health care decisions for myself as long as I am able to do so and to revoke this declaration at any time.

(1)   The following are my feelings and wishes regarding my health care (you may state the circumstances under which this declaration applies):

(2)   I particularly want to have all appropriate health care that will help in the following ways (you may give instructions for care you do want):

(3)   I particularly do not want the following (you may list specific treatment you do not want in certain circumstances):

(4)   I particularly want to have the following kinds of life-sustaining treatment if I am diagnosed to have a terminal condition (you may list the specific types of life-sustaining treatment that you want if you have a terminal condition):

(5) I particularly do not want the following kinds of life-sustaining treatment if I am diagnosed to have a terminal condition (you may list the specific types of life-sustaining treatment that you do not want if you have a terminal condition):

(6) I recognize that if I reject artificially administered sustenance, then I may die of dehydration or malnutrition rather than from my illness or injury. The following are my feelings and wishes regarding artificially administered sustenance should I have a terminal condition (you may indicate whether you wish to receive food and fluids given to you in some other way than by mouth if you have a terminal condition):

(7) Thoughts I feel are relevant to my instructions. (You may, but need not, give your religious beliefs, philosophy, or other personal values that you feel are important. You may also state preferences concerning the location of your care.)

(8) Proxy Designation. (If you wish, you may name someone to see that your wishes are carried out, but you do not have to do this. You may also name a proxy without including specific instructions regarding your care. If you name a proxy, you should discuss your wishes with that person.)

If I become unable to communicate my instructions, I designate the following person(s) to act on my behalf consistently with my instructions, if any, as stated in this document. Unless I write instructions that limit my proxy's authority, my proxy has full power and authority to make health care decisions for me. If a guardian or conservator of the person is to be appointed for me, I nominate my proxy named in this document to act as guardian or conservator of my person.

Name: _____

Address: _____

Phone Number: _____

Relationship (if any): _____

If the person I have named above refuses or is unable or unavailable to act on my behalf, or if I revoke that person's authority to act as my proxy, I authorize the following person to do so:

Name: _____

Address: _____

Phone Number: _____

Relationship (if any): _____

I understand that I have the right to revoke the appointment of the persons named above to act on my behalf at any time by communicating that decision to the proxy or my health care provider.

DATE: _____

SIGNED: _____

STATE OF _____

COUNTY OF _____

Subscribed, sworn to, and acknowledged before me by _____

on this _____ day of _____, 19 _____

_____

Notary Public

OR

(Sign and date here in the presence of two adult witnesses, neither of whom is entitled to any part of your estate under a will or by operation of law, and neither of whom is your proxy.)

I certify that the declarant voluntarily signed this declaration in my presence and that the declarant is personally known to me. I am not named as a proxy by the declaration, and to the best of my knowledge, I am not entitled to any part of the estate of the declarant under a will or by operation of law.

Witness _____ Address _____
Witness _____ Address _____

Sample Responses to the Minnesota Health-Care Declaration

The following are feelings and wishes regarding my health care (you may state the circumstances under which this declaration applies).

Sample A. "This declaration applies when I have an incurable or irreversible health condition with no reasonable hope of recovery. I trust the judgment of my designated proxy and want her or his decisions to be respected and followed."

Sample B. "This declaration applies when I have been diagnosed to have a terminal condition and can no longer make decisions for myself. In case of an injury or illness diagnosed as nonterminal I wish to be treated with all reasonable procedures."

I particularly want to have all appropriate health care that will help in the following ways (you may give instructions for care you do want):

Sample A. "I want narcotics or other pain medications given to me in the amount and by the means necessary to bring relief from pain."

Sample B. "I believe in the sanctity of life and would want all procedures used that might extend my life."

I particularly do not want the following:

Sample A "I do not want any treatment that will not help me recover or comfort me and will only prolong the dying process."

I particularly want to have the following kinds of life-sustaining treatment if I am diagnosed with a terminal condition.

Sample A. "If life-sustaining treatment has been initiated and it becomes apparent that further treatment is futile and is just prolonging death, treatment should be withdrawn."

Sample B. "If I am diagnosed with a terminal condition, I would want artificial food and hydration to be continued."

I particularly do not want the following kinds of life-sustaining treatment if I am diagnosed to have a terminal condition (you may list the specific types of life-sustaining treatment that you do not want if you have a terminal condition):

Sample A. "I would not want any medical treatment that prolongs my dying *and is not necessary for comfort*. If I am without feeling, thought, or awareness, if my neocortical brain is no longer functioning, if I am permanently unconscious, I direct my doctors to withhold or withdraw all life-sustaining treatment, including but not limited to a ventilator, supplemental oxygen, medication including antibiotics, and cardiopulmonary resuscitation."

I recognize that if I reject artificially administered sustenance, then I may die of dehydration or malnutrition rather than from my illness or injury. The following are my feelings and wishes regarding artificially administered sustenance should I have a terminal condition:

Sample A. "I consider artificial food and hydration a medical procedure and would want it withheld or withdrawn if my condition was considered futile and it would only prolong my dying."

Sample B. "I would want artificial food and hydration administered."

Thoughts I feel are relevant to my instructions (you may, but need not, give your religious beliefs, philosophy, or other personal values that you feel are important. You may also state preferences concerning the location of your care):

Sample A. "I would prefer to die at home unless my proxy deems it more appropriate for my comfort—or for other's comfort—that I be elsewhere. I value having those I love around me and would want the atmosphere to be warm, caring, and music-filled. I imagine an aura of expectation and appreciation of the richness and mystery of the moment."

Sample B. "I want to continue living as long as I am capable of enjoying life. If I lose my enjoyment of life and, in the opinion of my primary care physician, have no reasonable prospects of regaining it, I do not care to continue living."

Minnesota Durable Power of Attorney for Health Care Form

I, born on _____,
appoint _____ as my agent (attorney in fact)
to make any health care decision for me when, in the judgment of my attending physician, I am
unable to make or communicate the decision myself and my agent consents to make or communicate the decision on my behalf. In the event _____
is unable, unavailable, or unwilling to act as my agent, I appoint _____
as my alternative agent. My agent or any alternative agent has the power to make any health care
decision for me. This power includes the power to give consent, to refuse consent, or to withdraw
consent to any care, treatment, service, or procedure to maintain, diagnose, or treat my physical or
mental condition, including giving me food or water by artificial means. My agent or any alternative agent has the power, where consistent with the laws of this state, to make a health care
decision to withhold or stop health care necessary to keep me alive. It is my intention that my
agent or any alternative agent has a personal obligation to me to make health care decisions for me
consistent with my expressed wishes. I understand, however, that my agent or any alternative
agent has no legal duty to act.

My agent and any alternative agent have consented to act as my agent. My agent and any alternative agent have been notified that they will be nominated as a guardian or conservator for health
care decisions for me.

My agent or any alternative agent must act consistently with my desires as stated in this document or as otherwise made known by me to my agent or any alternative agent.

My agent or any alternative agent has the same rights as I would have to receive, review, and
obtain copies of my medical records and to consent to disclosure of those records.

In Witness Whereof I have hereunto signed my name this _____ day
of _____, 19 _____.

_____
(Signature of Principal)

STATE OF MINNESOTA
County of _____
The foregoing instrument was acknowledged before me this _____ day of _____,
19 _____, by _____.
(Insert Name of Principal)

_____
(Signature of Notary Public or Other Official)

or

I certify that in my presence, on the date appearing above, the principal, _____,
signed this instrument. I am not named as agent or alternative agent in the instrument.

Witness _____ Residing at _____
Witness _____ Residing at _____

Appendix F

State Agencies for Living Will Information

(Ask for your state legal service developer.)

Alabama	Alabama Commission on Aging	205-242-5743
Alaska	Older Alaskans Commission	907-465-3250
Arizona	Aging and Adult Administration	602-542-4446
Arkansas	Division of Aging and Adult Services	501-682-2441
	Department of Human Resources	800-950-5817 x118
California	Department of Aging	916-322-0488
Colorado	Aging and Adult Service	303-866-3851
	Legal Center	800-288-1376
Connecticut	Department of Aging	203-566-3238
Delaware	Division on Aging	302-577-4991
District of Columbia	Office on Aging	202-724-5622
	Legal Counsel for the Elderly	202-234-0970
Florida	Department of Elder Affairs	904-922-5297
Georgia	Office of Aging	404-657-5328
Hawaii	Executive Office on Aging	808-586-0100
Idaho	Office on Aging	208-334-3833 208-334-2220
Illinois	Department on Aging	217-785-2870 217-524-7945
Indiana	Division of Aging and Rehabilitation	317-232-7148
Iowa	Department of Elder Affairs	515-281-4657
Kansas	Department on Aging	913-296-4986
Kentucky	Division of Aging Services	502-564-6930
	Cabinet for Human Resources	502-564-7362
Louisiana	Office of Elderly Affairs	504-925-1700
Maine	Bureau of Elder and Adult Services	207-624-5335
Maryland	Office on Aging	410-225-1100 800-243-3425
Massachusetts	Executive Office of Elder Affairs	617-727-7750
Michigan	Office of Services to the Aging	517-373-4076
Minnesota	Board on Aging	612-296-0378 612-296-2770
Mississippi	Council on Aging	601-359-6764
Missouri	Division on Aging	314-751-3082
Montana	Department of Family Services	406-444-5900
	Office on Aging	406-444-3111
Nebraska	Department on Aging	402-471-2306

Nevada	Division of Aging Services	702-486-3545
New Hampshire	Division of Elderly and Adult Services	603-271-4690
New Jersey	Department of Community Affairs	609-633-6609
		609-292-4833
New Mexico	State Agency on Aging	505-827-7640
New York	State Office for the Aging	518-474-0608
		518-474-4425
North Carolina	Division of Aging	919-733-8400
		919-733-3983
North Dakota	Aging Services Division	701-224-2577
Ohio	Department of Aging	614-466-5500
		614-466-6598
Oklahoma	Aging Services Division	405-521-2327
	Special Unit on Aging	405-521-2281
Oregon	Senior and Disabled Services	503-945-6401
		503-378-4728
Pennsylvania	Department of Aging	717-783-1550
		717-783-6007
Rhode Island	Department of Elderly Affairs	401-277-2894
		401-277-2858
South Carolina	Division on Aging	803-737-7500
South Dakota	Office of Adult Services and Aging	605-773-3656
Tennessee	Commission on Aging	615-741-2056
Texas	Department on Aging	512-424-2757
Utah	Older Americans Advocacy Assistance	801-328-8891
	Division of Aging and Adult Services	801-538-3901
Vermont	Aging and Disabilities	802-241-2400
	Senior Citizens Law Project	802-748-8721
Virginia	Department for the Aging	804-371-8381
Washington	Aging and Adult Services Administration	206-586-3768
		206-493-4984
West Virginia	Commission on Aging	304-558-3317
Wisconsin	Bureau on Aging	608-266-2568
Wyoming	Older Americans Advocacy Program	307-632-9067
	Commission on Aging	307-777-7986

Select Bibliography

American Association of Retired Persons. *Tomorrow's Choices: Planning for Difficult Times.* Washington, D.C.: AARP Program Department, 1988.

American Medical Association. *Opinion of the AMA Council on Ethical and Judicial Affairs,* Chicago, IL, 15 March 1986.

Appelbaum, P. S., and L. H. Roth. "Clinical Issues in the Assessment of Competency." *American Journal of Psychiatry* 138 (1981): 1462-67.

Battin, Margaret P. "Euthanasia: The Way We Do It, the Way They Do It." *Journal of Pain and Symptom Management* 6, no. 5 (July 1991).

Beauvoir, Simone de. *Adieux: A Farewell to Sartre.* New York: Pantheon Books, 1984.

Bingham, J. *Courage to Change.* New York: Charles Scribner's Sons, 1972.

Borysenko, Joan. *Minding the Body, Mending the Mind.* New York: Bantam Books, 1987.

Brantner, John. Speech to Senior Workers Association, Minneapolis, MN, 1981.

Brescia, F. J. "Killing the Known Dying: Notes of a Death Watcher." *Journal of Pain and Symptom Management* 6, no. 5 (July 1991): 33.

Butler, Robert N., and Myrna Lewis. *Aging and Mental Health: Positive Psychosocial Approaches.* Saint Louis: C. V. Mosby, 1977.

Clemente, C. D. Anatomy: *A Regional Atlas of the Human Body.* 3d ed. Baltimore: Urban and Schwarzenberg, 1987.

Cohen, M. "Caring for Ourselves Can Be Funny Business." *Holistic Nurse Practice* (Aspen) 4, no. 4 (1989): 5.

Colby, William H. "Missouri Stands Alone." *Hastings Center Report* 20, no. 5 (September-October 1990): 5.

Cope, L. "Panel Says Doctors Ethically Can Help the Terminally Ill to Commit Suicide." *Minneapolis Star Tribune,* 30 March 1989.

Cousins, Norman. *Head First: The Biology of Hope.* New York: E. P. Dutton, 1989.

    "The Right to Die." *Saturday Review,* 14 June 1975.

    Human Options: An Autobiographical Notebook. New York: W. W. Norton, 1981.

Cowley, Malcolm. *The View from Eighty.* New York: Penguin Books, 1982.

Daumal, Rene. Mount Analogue. New York: Pantheon, 1959.

Dewey, J. *Experience and Education.* New York: Macmillan, 1938.

————. *Human Nature and Conduct.* New York: H. Holt and Co., 1922.

Dossey, Larry. *Recovering the Soul.* New York: Bantam Books, 1989.

Doyle, D., G. W. C. Hanks, and N. MacDonald. *Oxford Textbook of Palliative Medicine.* Oxford: Oxford University Press, 1993.

Durant, Will. *Pleasures of Philosophy.* New York: Simon and Schuster, 1953.

Ellison, Jerome. *Life's Second Half: The Pleasure of Aging.* Greenwich, Conn.: Devin-Adair Co., 1978.

Erikson, Erik. *Vital Involvement in Old Age.* New York: Norton, 1985.

Erikson, Erik, and Helen Kivnick. *Childhood and Society.* New York: Norton, 1963.

Evans, A. L., and B. A. Brody. "The Do-Not-Resuscitate Order in Teaching Hospitals." *Journal of the American Medical Association* 253, no. 15 (19 April 1985): 2236-39.

Fabry, Joseph. *Guideposts to Meaning: Discovering What Really Matters.* Oakland, Calif.: New Harbinger Publications, 1988.

"Focus: Living Wills." *Good Age,* March/April 1991, 5-8.

Frankl, Victor. *The Will to Meaning: Foundations and Applications of Logotherapy.* New York: New American Library, 1969.

Fusgen, I., and J. D. Summa. "How Much Sense Is There To Resuscitate An Aged Person?" *Gerontology* 24 (1978): 37.

Goldstein, D. A., and M. H. Antoni. "The Distribution of Repressive Coping Styles Among Nonmetastatic and Metastatic Breast Cancer Patients as Compared to Noncancer Control." *Journal of Psychology and Health* 3 (1989): 245-58.

Goodheart, Annette. "Laugh Your Way to Health." *Science of the Mind,* September 1988, 15.

Greer, S., and T. Morris. "Psychological Attributes of Women Who Develop Breast Cancer: A Controlled Study." *Journal of Psychosomatic Research* 19, no. 2 (1975): 147-53.

Herbert, Trish. "The Most Courageous of All." *Minnesota Sun Publications,* 16 February 1987.

Humphrey, Derek. *Final Exit.* Secaucus, N.J.: Carol Publishing, 1991.

Inskip, Leonard. "Treating Body-Mind." *Minneapolis Star Tribune,* 4 August 1991.

Jevne, Ronna Fay, and Alexander Levitan. *No Time for Nonsense.* San Diego, Calif.: LuraMedia, 1989.

Kanin, Garson. *It Takes a Long Time to Become Young.* New York: Doubleday, 1978.

Keirsey, David, and Marilyn Bates. *Please Understand Me.* Del Mar, Calif.: Prometheus Nemesis Book Co., 1984.

Kobasa, S., and M. Puccetti. "Personality and Social Resources in Stress Resistance." *Journal of Personality and Social Psychology* 45, no. 4 (1983).

LaFave, L., et al. "Superiority, Enhanced Self-esteem, and Perceived Incongruity Humor Theory." In *Humour and Laughter: Theory Research and Applications,* edited by A. Chapman and H. Foot. New York: Wiley, 1976.

LeSeuer, Meridel. *Ripenings: Selected Works, 1927-1980.* Old Westbury, N.Y.: The Feminist Press, 1982.

Levine, Stephen. *Healing into Life and Death.* Garden City, N.Y.: Anchor Press/Doubleday, 1987.

Lopez, Barry. Crossing *Open Ground.* New York: Random House, Vintage Books, 1989.

Luks, Allan, and Peggy Payne. *The Healing Power of Doing Good.* New York: Fawcett Columbine, 1991.

Lynn, Joanne, and James F. Childress. "Must Patients Always Be Given Food and Water?" *The Hastings Center Report* 13, no. 5 (October 1983): 17-21.

Nagel, E. L. "Complications of CPR." *Critical Care Medicine* 9, no. 5 (1981): 424.

Newman, M., and B. Berkowitz. *How to Take Charge of Your Life.* New York: Bantam Books, 1977.

Nouwen, Henri. *Reaching Out: The Three Movements of Spiritual Life.* Garden City, N.Y.: Doubleday, 1975.

O'Regan, Brandon, ed. "Mind and Body: Pathways of Linkage." *Institute of Noetic Sciences Newsletter,* Spring 1986.

Ornish, Dean. *Dr. Dean Ornish's Program for Reversing Heart Disease.* New York: Random House, 1990.

Orsello, Jean K. *Planning for Incapacity.* St. Paul: Minnesota Adult Protection Coalition, 1990.

Parkes, Colin Murray. *Bereavement: Studies of Grief in Adult Life*. New York: International Universities Press, 1972.

Pert, Candice B. "The Wisdom of the Receptors: Neuropeptides, the Emotions, and the Bodymind," *Advances: Institute for Advancement of Health* 3, no. 3 (Summer 1986): 8-16.

Peseschkian, Nossrat. *In Search of Meaning: A Psychotherapy of Small Steps*. New York: Springer-Verlag, Bellins, 1985.

President's Commission for the Study of Ethical Problems in Medicine and Biomedical and Behavioral Research. *Defining Death*. Washington, D.C.: GPO, 1981.

President's Commission for the Study of Ethical Problems in Medicine and Biomedical and Behavioral Research. "Uniform Determination of Death Act (UDDA)." *In Deciding to Forego Life-Sustaining Treatment: Ethical, Medical, and Legal Issues in Treatment Decisions*. Washington, D.C.: GPO, 1983.

Rattenburg, J. "Mind-Body Mania." *Vegetarian Times*, November 1993, 75-79.

Rossi, Ernest. *The Psychobiology of Mind-Body Healing*. New York: W. W. Norton, 1986.

Scofield, G. "Privacy (or Liberty) and Assisted Suicide." *Journal of Pain and Symptom Management* 6, no. 5 (July 1991).

Seligman, Martin E. Learned Optimism. New York: Alfred A. Knopf, 1990.

Severance, Janet. "Predictors of Elderly Participation in Long-term Care Decision-making." University of Minnesota, Department of Sociology, 1988.

Siegler, M. "Does 'Doing Everything' Include CPR?" *Hastings Center Report* 12, no. 5 (October 1982): 27.

Simonton, Stephanie Matthew. *The Healing Family*. New York: Bantam Books, 1989.

Slovut, Gordon. "They'd Give High Doses of Pain-killers to Dying, Doctors Say." *Minneapolis Star Tribune*, 26 April 1990.

Spiegel, David, Jean Bloom, Helena C. Kraemer, and Ellen Gottheil. "Effect of Psychosocial Treatment on Survival of Patients with Metastatic Breast Cancer." *Lancet*, 14 October 1989, 888-91.

Spiegel, David, Jean Bloom, I. D. Yalom, et al. "Group Support for Patients with Metastatic Breast Cancer." *Arch Gen Psychiatry* 38, no. 5 (1981): 527.

U.S. Department of Health and Human Services. Division of Organ Transplantation. *Organ Transplantation*. Publication no. (HRS-M-SP) 89-1. Washington, D.C., October 1988.

Veatch, Robert M. "Commentary." *Hastings Center Report* 12, no. 5 (1982): 45.

Wanser, S. H., S. J. Adelstein, and R. E. Cranford. "The Physicians's Responsibility Toward Hopelessly Ill Patients." *The New England Journal of Medicine* 310, no. 15 (1984): 955-59.

"Who Can Afford a Nursing Home?" *Consumer Reports* 53, no. 5. (May 1988).

Wolfe, Warren. "Man Would Refuse Ruling to Take Wife Off Respirator." *Minneapolis Star Tribune*, 29 May 1991.

Worsnop, R. L. "Transplants: Why Demand Exceeds Supply." *Editorial Research Report* 1, no. 27 (5 October 1990).

Zerwekh, J. V. "The Dehydration Question." *Nursing*, January 1983, 41-51.

DATE DUE

GAYLORD			PRINTED IN U.S.A.